Mary & Peter
Fond memorie
Love · Mar —

HIRTH

G000168174

"WHILE MY HEART BEATS..."

The Seán Devereux Story

1964 ~ 1993

THE DEVEREUX FAMILY

Pen Press Publishers Ltd
London

First published in Great Britain by
Pen Press Publishers Ltd
39-41, North Road
Islington
London N7 9DP

ISBN 1 900796 49 X

Printed and bound in the UK by
Antony Rowe Ltd
Chippenham, Wilts

A catalogue record of this book is available
from the British Library

Cover photograph by Michael Emery

Cover design by Catrina Sherlock

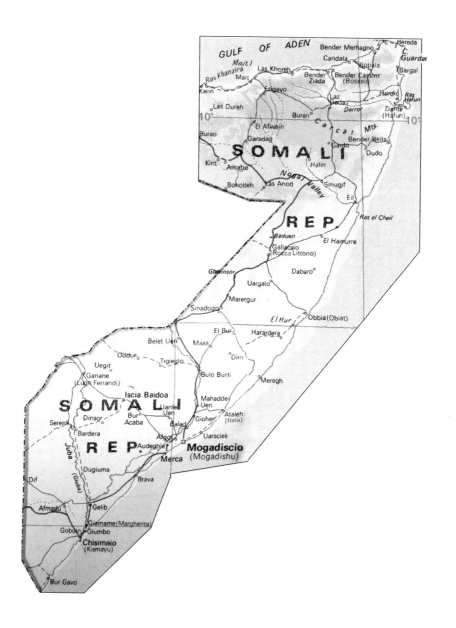

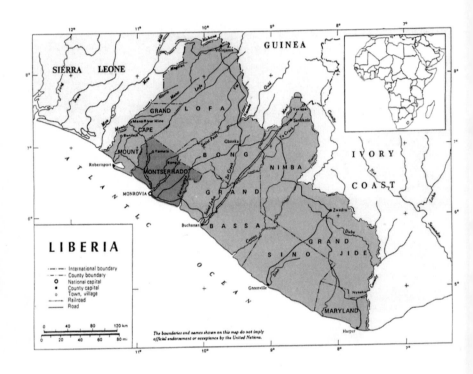

SIERRA LEONE

GUINEA

GRAND

LOFA

CAPE

Mano River Mine
Bomi
Bopolu

MOUNT

Robertsport

MONTSERRADO

MONROVIA

BONG

Gbanga

NIMBA

Sanokole

ATLANTIC

GRAND

BASSA

IVORY

COAST

Buchanan

Zwedru

GRAND

Tebe

GRAND

SINO

JIDE

OCEAN

Greenville

Nyaake

MARYLAND

Harper

LIBERIA

- - · - - International boundary
- - - - County boundary
- ○ National capital
- ● County capital
- ○ Town, village
- ＋＋＋ Railroad
- —— Road

0   40   80   120 km
0   20   40   60   80 mi.

'While my heart beats I have to do what I think I can do – and that is to help those who are less fortunate ...'
Seán Devereux

DEDICATION

In memory of Seán and Dermot.

For the people and children of Africa, that they may be united in peace, freedom and love.

ACKNOWLEDGEMENTS

Encouragement to write Seán's story came from many sources. We were mainly inspired by Seán's father, the late Dermot Devereux.

Our deepest thanks go to John Sweeney of *The Observer*, for his invaluable guidance and support, and to our editor Linda Lloyd, who pieced the jigsaw together.

A special thank you to Father Gerrard Hughes for his encouragement and advice.

Deep gratitude to all our family and friends for never failing to love and support us. We especially want to thank:
Michael Emery
Caroline Tanner
Mary Considene
Ofeiba Quist-Arcton

We would like to thank many of the aid workers for their kindness.

Thanks also to Peter Kosminski, director of the Yorkshire Television documentary 'The Dying of the Light', his researcher, Emma Wallace, and Richard Alwyn, producer of the Everyman film 'Mr Seán'.

Heartfelt thanks to the Salesian community for their support.

THE SEÁN DEVEREUX CHILDREN'S FUND

Seán's great love of children was what initially led him to Africa. He wanted to give them the same opportunities he had been given. He saw great hope for Africa in its children; they were the future and, with his help, they could make the world a better place.

With this wish in mind, the Seán Devereux Children's Fund was established. All proceeds from the sale of this book go to the fund.

Reg. Charity No. 1057777

DO NOT GO GENTLE INTO THAT GOOD NIGHT

Do not go gentle into that good night,
Old age should burn and rave at close of day;
Rage, rage against the dying of the light.

Though wise men at their end know dark is right,
Because their words have forked no lightning they
Do not go gentle into that good night.

Good men, the last wave by, crying how bright
Their frail deeds might have danced in a green bay,
Rage, rage against the dying of the light.

Wild men who caught and sang the sun in flight,
And learn, too late, they grieved it on its way,
Do not go gentle into that good night.

Grave men, near death, who see with blinding sight
Blind eyes could blaze like meteors and be gay,
Rage, rage against the dying of the light.

And you, my father, there on the sad height,
Curse, bless me now with your fierce tears, I pray.
Do not go gentle into that good night.
Rage, rage against the dying of the light.

Dylan Thomas

It is not the length
of existence
that counts.

But what is achieved
during that existence
however short.

Dear Mr & Mrs Devereux & Daughters, 22-2-93

The enclosed has taken rather longer to reach you than planned because when I removed it from above my inglenook, where it has hung for many-a-year, I discovered the frame needed replacing.

I saw you on television Mr Devereux and read about your courageous, selfless son Seán who cared so much for others.

I hope therefore, you will accept it with the love intended. Perhaps one day, at present beyond your view, it might just bring you some small measure of comfort.

I pray that it will.

Sincerely yours,
Nicola

FOREWORD

Seán Devereux wasn't a saint. He was an ordinary man who did something extraordinary with his life. He was bubbling with fun, making jokes, inventing elaborate practical jokes, comforting the afflicted and afflicting the comfortable. But the abiding impression you get from people who met him was he was such fun to be with. Once, in Liberia, he was beaten up by some armed thugs who stole the contents of an aid lorry – destined for starving children – from him. He was badly knocked about, and his best friend Michael Emery rushed to see how he was. Emery was greeted by a zombie, lying prone on his bed, entirely swaddled in bandages. Seán looked like the Mummy in a bad horror movie. Emery was aghast, and then he realised that the Mummy, far from being immobile, was shaking. Seán was shaking with laughter. He had turned an ugly and terrifying moment of savagery in Africa into a joke. That takes extraordinary courage, and a love of life, and a determination not to be overcome by the forces of evil.

I first came across the story of Seán after he had been killed. A BBC TV news bulletin showed Dermot 'Gerry' Devereux, Maureen, Theresa and Tania standing by the gate of their lovely home in Hampshire, White Picketts, mired in misery. I was instantly and profoundly touched by their loss, and I determined to do the story for *The Observer* magazine. It was one of the most terrible and enriching assignments that I have ever done. Terrible, because of the profound sense of loss everyone who had ever met Seán conveyed to me. Enriching, because he was a wonderful, fantastic force for good, for standing up for the underdog, for caring about the wretched of the earth. I was privileged to get to know Dermot and Maureen and the rest of the family. After the article in *The Observer* magazine appeared, the film-maker Peter Kosminski read it and decided to make a film of Seán's life. Dermot and Maureen – the souls of hospitality – gave a dinner party to thank myself and *Observer* photographer Roger Hutchings. I found the dinner wonderful and unbearably sad, at the same time, and dealt with my distress by sloshing back too much white wine. Then, to my eternal shame, I fell asleep, my face plum down in the strawberry pavlova. After half an hour's unusual kip, I woke up and apologised repeatedly. A year and a half later I was in a car, driving into northern Bihac in Bosnia. The road was tense, the atmosphere grim. Bullets had been flying moments before. And then the aid worker sitting next to me, one Victor Tanner – a great friend of Seán's – looked at me and said: 'I know who you are. You're the bloke who fell asleep into the Devereux's strawberry pavlova.' Instantly, the mood in the car changed from suppressed terror to wonderful hilarity. It was as if Seán was in the car with us.

Time moved on, and cancer finally got Dermot – after a determined battle on his part. So the story you are about to read is a double tragedy, of two men, taken from us long before their time. And yet there are moments in this book which will have you weeping with laughter and glorying in the good fight being fought.

Never confuse solemnity with seriousness. Seán was a laugh, sure. But he was deadly serious about the misery of children in the third world who suffered from the arms trade. Through his energy and commitment, he diverted their minds from the power of the gun. His magic bag of conjuring tricks enabled children to relive their stolen childhood. His love of sport gave them back their self-esteem and dared them to hope again.

He shielded the terrorised local people through his presence and most of all through his honest voice, speaking out the truth in a wilderness of untold suffering. He witnessed their dreams being washed away in a sea of blood. His anger intensified because the innocent were being used as cannon fodder in senseless conflicts: their world obliterated by the horrors of war, our world secure and enriched by the arms trade which so blindly sustains our economy and enables us to live whilst others die. The malaise of our own people, confused by their own cleverness, deepens day by day.

But our sleep will be eased because we inject aid workers like Seán into troubled lands, enabling our elected governments to continue fanning the flames of conflict – for where there is money there is a killing to be made.

Seán learnt the power of the Western war machine in the Third World, not through abstract propaganda and abstruse polemic, but through direct painful and ultimately fatal personal experience.

He raged against the machine, but he never lost his humanity or his sense of fun. The kids of Africa sensed his greatness.

They called him Mr Seán.

John Sweeney

PROLOGUE

Freetown, Sierra Leone, 1992

'So long now, Dad!' He was laughing as he grasped my hand, gripping me in a bear hug, a farewell gesture that had become more frequent these recent years. No words were spoken yet a thousand passed between us. Then the moment with its inexplicable spiritual dimension was over.

'Mr Seán, Mr Seán let's go, let's go now.'

I watched him as he moved away, clutched by small black hands and harangued by what seemed like a multitude of young voices. I felt tears forcing their way to my eyes.

I had stood before at the close of an African evening and was familiar with the warmth of the evening breeze, the glow of the sinking sun, the smell of Jacaranda trees, the daylight sounds giving way to the distinctive sounds of the night. But somehow it was different this time.

He was a little distant from me now, his figure silhouetted against the sun: the familiar blue knee-length shorts, brown leather sandals, the baggy T-shirt, complete with baseball cap made from African straw. The small barefooted children chattered and skipped alongside him as they sent tiny dust clouds into the air from the Murrum Road. His suitcase was perched on the head of an older boy. He was submerged in the laughter of his new-found friends who had taken my place.

They crossed the small hill in tandem with the sinking sun, moving out of sight as if they were merging into the African landscape. Lost, lost now, forever, I told myself. Seán had vanished, it seemed, into the heart of Africa and its people. I turned and walked towards the waiting plane with a feeling of overwhelming anguish. The aircraft was soon airborne, gaining altitude and banking over the scorched earth below. I scanned the savannah, hoping that I might catch sight of him once more, but he was gone, on a journey which would change both his life and the lives of all of us at home.

This strange feeling of loss occupied my mind for several hours. I have reflected on that parting scene so many times since. Was this man, bursting with energy, humour and infectious passion for life, the same son we had known and loved for 27 years? I felt an immense pride in the work he was doing in Africa. Yet why this great sadness?

It was perhaps a foreshadowing of the event, just one year later, which would shatter our lives forever. In the Somalian port city of Kismayo on 2 January 1993, Seán was killed by three bullets from a Kalashnikov rifle. It was one of the many weapons supplied by the civilised world.

In the name of civilisation we send young people like Seán to do humanitarian work in the worst places on earth. Somalia was such a place, a country that was tearing itself apart with the arms so easily available to its savage warlords. We supplied the weaponry that was to massacre thousands of innocent men and women, to dragoon children as young as eight or nine into becoming armed fighters.

Seán lost his life because he dared to speak out against such wild and senseless injustices.

DERMOT:
SOMALIA REVISITED

The aircraft touched down in Nairobi at 3.30 in the morning. It was 6 May 1993. There was something unreal about that moment as I walked towards the two waiting figures at the other end of the aircraft jetty, Mark Sterling, Seán's boss at UNICEF, and Bill Condey, UNICEF Somalia Security chief.

I could hear Seán's laughter as he had bantered with Sterling, the same laughter I'd heard on the last day of December 1992, when we all said goodbye to him – his mother Maureen, Theresa and Tania, his two sisters, and me. The air was hot and sticky as it had been that day. There were tears in my eyes then, but the burning I felt in them now was for a very different reason.

The two figures ahead of me misted over and their outlines blurred. My head seemed to be crushed between a vice, my stomach knotted in merciless pain. The voices of airline personnel, colleagues I had known for many years, called my name in greeting. I raised my hand, but saw no-one as they passed me.

I reached the end of the jetty and accepted Mark's outstretched hand. He is an Australian in his late thirties, a good six-footer, well built, and would have made a fine rugby forward. His short cropped hair made him look younger than his years. Mark was casually dressed, but his normal relaxed manner was shrouded in a tense, uneasy look. His face revealed the anxiety he felt at meeting me again in very different circumstances. I felt I knew what he was thinking. The questions hung in the air, unspoken. Could the United Nations have done more? Would Seán still be alive if the UN had pulled all of them out of Kismayo when things deteriorated to such an extent? Why hadn't UNICEF, Seán's agency, been more vigilant? Why had they not responded more quickly to Seán's plea to send in more money to keep the gunmen at bay? Had UNICEF expected too much of these young people caught up in such chaos?

We stood there frozen, unable to speak.

Bill stepped forward and placed his hand on my shoulder. 'It's a bastard,' he said. 'It's a bastard.' He looked me straight in the eye, his brown eyes piercing mine, willing me to hold back the tears.

3

Bill was a Scot, a former officer in the SAS and a security officer with a gentleness underlying his exterior toughness. He held my hand firmly and said: 'Seán was a great man. We will get the bastard responsible if it's the last thing we do.'

He was dwarfed by the tall figure of Mark behind him, but his stature grew as his words somehow sustained me. I felt a surge of energy to keep going because I knew he cared. He had respected Seán. I knew he would help me in my quest for justice. Somewhere in the darkness of my own soul he touched that misplaced desire to avenge Seán's death and settle the score. But I also knew that the sanctity of life meant more to Seán than revenge.

An eight-seater UNICEF aircraft was standing by to fly me across to Kismayo and then on to Mogadishu to the headquarters of Admiral Jonathan Howe, the American head of the UN military mission in Somalia. We were due to leave just after 5 am. Bill took care of my passport and by-passed the immigration formalities. We proceeded to a small ante-room at the end of the airport building. I sat there gazing through the windows at the UNICEF aircraft as dawn broke and the sun rose on the other side of the plane. One or two Africans were refuelling while others hurriedly carried out checks on the aircraft. A new day dawned. I thought: 'Life goes on!' I couldn't help hearing Seán say: 'There's a long day ahead, Dad. Things have to be done and we have to get on with it.'

Mark was back in the room holding a couple of cups of coffee. He had not just been Seán's boss, but his friend too.

'You know what I feel about Seán,' he said. 'There are no words. I can't tell you how much this has affected all of us here. He was such a bloody wonderful person.'

He paused, then asked: 'How's the rest of the family?'

'They're reasonable,' I said, 'coping, day by day. They're being very brave. None of us can believe this has happened, Mark.'

He dropped his head and moved towards the window, silent now, and looking out at the empty sky. He turned towards me. 'I can't tell you how much I appreciate you coming here. It's not going to be an easy day.'

He explained that there would be six of us: Mark; myself; Bill; Gerry McCrudden, the First Secretary at British High Commission in Nairobi; Scott Peterson, the East Africa correspondent of *The Daily Telegraph* and a friend of Seán's; and Ann Wright of the US State Department who was special adviser to Admiral Howe.

At 4.30 am the other three joined us in the departure room. Gerry McCrudden was the first to grasp my hand and offer his deep condolences, followed by the others. Gerry said that he was representing the High

4

Commission and would be available to give me all the assistance possible. He was unlike the other First Secretaries I had met in the past. His warm, friendly Irish disposition made him easy to be with, but behind the relaxed easy-going personality was a sharp, alert mind. Ann Wright explained that she was part of the UNISOM team and was principally responsible for setting up a judiciary in Somalia under Admiral Howe.

I had met Scott Peterson a few months previously and had shared a few drinks with him and Seán. Scott was a young man in his early thirties who had been in East Africa for some time. Seán had met him during his visits to Kismayo and Mogadishu when Scott had stayed over at the UNICEF compound. They had got to know each other quite well. Like Seán, Scott had witnessed terrible acts of cruelty. He was an honest reporter who told it as it was, and Seán had respected his honesty and commitment to his work. He had taken many risks, determined to relay the story from the front line, recording terrible events as they unfolded. I was struck by the courage of Scott and the other young people who exposed themselves to all sorts of dangers to tell the world what was going on.

The condolences of the party made me think once again about Seán. His infectious passion for life had reached out to those whose lives were being denied. He wanted them to have the same opportunities as he had. I reminisced on earlier days when Seán was growing up and more recent times when he had helped me, his own father, through a personal crisis. He was, above all, my friend. I recalled all that he had encountered in the space of four short years in Liberia. It was as if he had already lived a full life. He was on a straight path like an arrow in flight before it fell to earth.

His life and death now unfolded in front of me as if in a nightmare. I was frightened, anxious, confused, caught in a cobweb suspended in some vast unoccupied space. Seán was gone; Seán had left something behind. He had impacted on the lives of others. I thought of the thousands of letters from the four corners of the earth which had filled our house after his death. These letters meant so much to me and my family; they were testimony that Seán and his story had changed the lives of others.

But Seán was no saint. He was stubborn, untidy, impatient. It had been hell to make him study when he was at school. His high spirits drove us mad from time to time. He was very masculine and often tried to dominate his sisters. His endless practical jokes frequently backfired, causing havoc. And latterly his assumption that the whole household was involved in the world aid programme left us exhausted. But he was so alive...

My thoughts were interrupted by Bill, who said that the aircraft was ready and we had the 'all clear' to depart for Kismayo. We were airborne by 5.15 am The two pilots told me they had flown Seán many times previously. Like all those I met during my time in Somalia, their depth of feeling regarding Seán's death really moved me.

The aircraft flew over the game reserves of Kenya as we headed towards the coastline, each one of us shrouded in our thoughts. The movement of the great elephants and wildebeest below reminded me that life was still rich and wonderful, but the familiar landscapes no longer engendered the excitement of happier times.

I remembered Seán at five years old. We had taken him on safari and I can still feel his elation and daring as he had tried to befriend a herd of African elephants. There was the day he made friends with some Masai children and wandered off into the bush, joining them in the task of herding the cattle and grazing them on the new green pastures. Fond memories flooded back of a five-year-old bartering, trading sunglasses and a T-shirt for water melons. Of the mutual intrigue between the small white boy and the willowy black children with mud-plaited hair and exotic tribal markings as they walked towards a watering hole, leaving his parents bewildered as to where on earth he had got to. Cattle and wildlife had gathered there to take advantage of the long-awaited rains. The children plunged into the water too, transcending all differences of colour, culture and creed as they splashed about. It was a glimpse of the world as it should be: just children at play out of the heat of the sun. The elephants stood downwind, their gaze occasionally turned to the crowd assembled at the water-hole as they raised their heads and flapped their bellow-like ears in the breeze.

This was the scene that greeted us. Seán was amidst his friends, standing on top of a large boulder near the pool and waving a brightly coloured Masai loin cloth to attract the distant elephants, encouraged by his companions who were shouting 'tembo, tembo' ('elephant, elephant'). Fortunately the elephants were too far away to see.

My stomach turned and sank as I allowed my mind to focus on the reality of the journey that lay ahead. Bill pressed a cup of coffee into my hand. The security situation was bad in both Kismayo and Mogadishu. 'We'll make our stay as brief as possible,' he said.

The Somalia coastline came into sight. I watched the pilot run through his pre-landing checks. I was willing the clock to turn back, hoping that Seán was down there below, alive, that somehow I could stand him up, and he could walk again, that all of this was a nightmare, and soon I would wake up.

As the aircraft taxied into the stand we were flanked on either side by UN trucks with heavily armed Belgian troops, conspicuous in their blue helmets. The aircraft door opened, allowing an oven-hot blast of air into the cabin. The sun was surprisingly high in the sky even though it was still just around seven in the morning. As we left the aircraft the hot rays seemed to dispel my tiredness. The airport comprised a small terminal building and control tower. Military vehicles were moving this way and that. The debris of damaged aircraft lay off the runways. The buildings were honeycombed from mortar fire. I stood motionless on the apron for a moment, surveying the dismal sight of Kismayo airport. A feeling of anger welled up inside me as I muttered: 'What a hell hole. All his energy and commitment for this.'

Once again Seán's voice was with me: 'That's it, Dad, your old negative self again. You'll go a long way with that.' Seán always tried to make sure that I focused on the positive when I questioned the usefulness of the aid programme and our country's involvement in Africa. He, of course, had no doubts about the contribution we could make through education and development. But he questioned the way in which we discharged our responsibility and the motivation behind our involvement. He recognised the value of African culture and guarded against forcing western values on a developing nation. There were times, too, when he wondered if we had done more harm than good. Nonetheless, he was firmly committed, enthusiastic and optimistic about the future.

'You have to keep moving,' Bill called, propelling me out of my reverie. 'If you stand still here you could wake up dead.'

'Dead or alive, what does it matter?' I thought. But then I got a grip of myself and realised the others were seated in the waiting vehicle. They were surrounded by an array of heavily armed blue helmets, our escorts. The lead vehicle had a high-tech machine gun mounted on the front, manned by four soldiers. Two trucks with fifteen men in each acted as outriders. The rear vehicle carried both machine and mortar guns. The UN troops were young, not much older than Seán. What a bloody life, I thought. These young people risking their lives – for what?

Our small convoy moved off quickly. The airport was soon behind and the road to Kismayo stretched out ahead. The hot wind helped to keep the flies at bay. The blue sky above acted as a backdrop to the fireball that was rising rapidly. It promised to be one of those dry, scorching days. The perspiration was running down my shoulder blades. Small wonder then that a steady flow of water was rolling down the face of the trooper next to me, soaking his shirt under the heat of his steel helmet. His automatic firearm was pointing out over my shoulder, his finger resting lightly on the firing mechanism. One pull of the trigger and a spray of bullets would be released into the air, killing everyone in front of it.

I reflected on Seán's words in his last letter from Somalia, when he spoke of the power of the gun and other weapons of destruction. The world had become an uncomfortable place. I was entering a country where thousands upon thousands of men had their own weapons, and were destroying the lifeblood of their own nation. I looked at the finger of the soldier holding the trigger of the gun and wondered whose hand had pulled the trigger on Seán. Tears started to burn my eyes again as I thought of his life ebbing away as he lay in the sand in this God-forsaken place. I was determined to find out who had killed him and who was ultimately responsible for his death. I needed to know why his voice had been silenced. I had to find out why he was killed after American forces had arrived to protect the aid workers and safeguard the humanitarian relief. Seán was with the military most of the day, agreeing with the commander the necessary support to effect the next day's operation. How could he have been shot down in such circumstances? Why was his driver or someone else not available to drive him back to the compound? Why was he allowed to walk the seven-minute distance unarmed, accompanied only by two Somalia aid workers? Why was there no military presence at the UNICEF compound? Why, four months later, was his killer still as free as a bird? Admiral Howe would have to shed light on these questions.

The sound of Mark Sterling's voice diverted my gaze away from the butt of the rifle. 'We'll take you to the feeding medical centres which Seán set up back in November,' he said. 'Then we'll look at the water project and displaced people's camps. Then on to the UNICEF compound to meet the UNICEF staff and some of the local people. We have a meeting with the Belgian Force Commander at 15 00 hrs. Hopefully we can fly you on the chopper up the Juba Valley to see the Bailey Bridge – it's now been completed and named after Seán. We'll need to be back at 17 00 hours for take-off to Mogadishu before dark. We're scheduled to meet Admiral Howe at 7.45 am.'

'OK, fine, fine,' I said. 'I– I'd like to see the place where Seán was—'

Mark cut me off: 'Of course, of course. We thought you would want your own private moment when we reach the UNICEF compound. It's very near the entrance.'

The Land Rover rode the bumps as we hit one dip after another. My head was thumping now, aggravated by the rough ride and the heat of the day. The countryside flipped by as we passed one devastated area after another. The landscape was flat, the bleakness broken up by what remained of dwellings scattered here and there. Goats ran across the road shepherded by a small boy who raised his stick in salute. A camel raised its head, munching a scorched piece of grass as the noise of the heavy trucks passed on either side in a cloud of dust. But that was it. No more evidence of life en route to the town. It was as if everyone had abandoned the land. I wondered how Seán had managed to keep his spirits up in a place such as this.

During our journey through the country the bright colour and smell of the acacia trees on either side of the road provided some relief from the barren terrain. Seán had always mentioned the pleasure of seeing these trees and how beautiful the country could be if energy was put into nurturing the land. 'A good irrigation system could make the world of difference here,' he had said.

As we approached the town, the ravages of fierce fighting became apparent. Not a single building was intact. Every piece of steel and timber had been ripped from the buildings. Telegraph poles had been cut down. The copper wire from the telephone wires had been looted. The town was simply a pile of rubble. Water and sanitation services were non-existent. People wandered aimlessly through the streets. No one took much notice of the armed convoy as we moved through Kismayo. There was an air of apathy about the place, as if everyone had given up.

I was struck by the quietness. I turned to Bill: 'It's remarkably peaceful,' I said. He made no comment, simply looked around as if expecting the next shell to fall. We came to a halt at the Medical Centre and Vaccination Clinic. A long line of women and children waited their turn to go forward and receive a jab in the arm or a few drops of liquid on the tongue. The maternity unit was empty. One of the Somali medical staff and two Swiss nurses were proud to show me the newly acquired delivery bench. Today would be someone's lucky day: at last there were medicines available for those in need.

We moved on quickly to the feeding centre, set up by Seán and Caroline Tanner. Caroline was a UNICEF nutritionist and an old friend of Seán's from Liberia. The two of them had worked together during the crazy civil war there in the early 1990s. In Kismayo they'd moved mountains to set up a number of feeding centres since their arrival in September 1992.

Little escaped Caroline's notice and she gave short shrift to bureaucracy. Her persistence and sharp mind did not always endear her to her superiors. However, she was well respected for her valuable contribution to the field of nutrition; Caroline had helped save many thousands of lives during her short stay in Liberia. She was married to fellow aid worker Victor Tanner and they had worked in many troubled parts of the world. In Somalia Victor was responsible for the co-ordination of the World Food Programme while Caroline worked with Seán setting up UNICEF feeding centres. Along with many others, the aid workers worked hard to fight off mass starvation. They made the difference.

The feeding centres were the only hope the people had. The construction was basic, a large, open-sided area with a makeshift roof made from large tarpaulin to shade the sun. Hundreds of women and children awaited their turn to receive their basic meal of rice and a meat-like substance. The food was prepared and consumed on site to ensure that each one was fed. Tiny children were clinging to my fingers, others hanging on to my legs. A number of the aid workers held the pitifully small bodies of underfed babies, weighing them in a bag suspended from a cord. Some of them were no heavier than a two-pound bag of sugar. Old people approached me, holding their shrunken faces in their hands, thanking me for the gift of food.

Mark appeared. 'Seán did a fantastic job here. The numbers at the feeding centre have been reduced by half, there are far fewer suffering from malnutrition, the vaccination programme has exceeded all expectations.'

As I moved around the various projects, I could feel Seán's energy. I imagined him working flat out as he always did, enjoying the challenge, constantly looking for ways to do more, encouraging others, laughing, teasing, taking the rise and eager for the next day which would bring something new.

'WHERE THERE'S LIFE, THERE'S HOPE'

The scene at the displaced people's camp was unbelievable. I gazed across the vast expanse, staring at the countless thousands of people sheltering beneath the blue and green dome-shaped tarpaulins, a sea of untold suffering.

Seán had been working on a project to resettle some 50 000 of these tent people back in their homes in the Lower Juba Valley region. He had devised a programme involving the distribution of food and clothing, together with a subsistence programme which would provide basic seed, rice and farming tools so that the people could look after themselves again. But it had been difficult to implement this plan prior to the arrival of the UN troops in Somalia. Seán and other relief workers in the country had routinely suffered harassment and death threats. But once the troops arrived, things would be different...

I could now understand why moving these people had been such a high priority for Seán. I could also make sense of his passionate commitment and his need to remain in Somalia until the job was done. I felt bad about my persistent complaints that he had done enough and given enough of himself in the three and a half years he'd spent in Liberia. I regretted that I had not done more when he told me about the risks involved and of the harassment he and others had been subjected to. I was angry with the ruthless warlords who persecuted their own people, massacred women and children, robbed and looted the humanitarian relief which Seán and the other aid workers were trying to deliver.

I was angry, too, that there had been no support and back-up for him and his team when the going got tough. In Somalia the UN was caught between the devil and the deep blue sea, but those in positions of accountability cannot be exonerated. It seems there was a high degree of abdication on the part of the UNICEF hierarchy in Somalia, as Seán and his fellow workers sank further into the quagmire in Kismayo. They were left in the main to their own devices as they struggled to fend off ruthless gunmen.

The gravity of the situation in Kismayo escaped those in the UNICEF

11

head office in Mogadishu as they too battled for survival. But they were not alone in their lack of support, for the UN military failed to grasp the magnitude of the situation in this city and provided no real measure of protection. It was hard to accept that my son had been killed at a time when the most sophisticated armed forces with the best intelligence in the world had been sent here expressly to protect people like him.

The arrival of the American troops should have heralded the end of the exploitation. No longer could the warlords go on persecuting the people. The rich pickings of humanitarian relief would no longer be available. Vast sums of money could no longer be extracted from aid workers for so-called 'protection'. The people would become strong again. Hope would be restored. But history has its own way of telling its story, for where there is money there is a killing to be made.

Seán and I had talked about this when I intercepted him in mid-November 1992, two months after he had moved from Liberia to Somalia. We'd arranged to meet at Wilson Airfield in Nairobi, as that day Seán and Mark Sterling were both due to fly out of Kismayo, the southern port in war-ravaged Somalia, where Seán was working for UNICEF. Kismayo had a truly horrible reputation: thousands of starving people were terrorised by the warlords' gunmen. Shortly after Seán's return to Kismayo the gunmen in their heavily armoured 'technicals' held up the UNICEF aid plane and robbed the pilots and passengers of all their belongings. The port was no better. On average, 80 per cent of the aid destined for the starving in the hinterland was looted by gunmen. Among international aid workers Kismayo was known as 'the city without mercy'.

That day I waited and waited. I had been told that they were scheduled to arrive on UNICEF One, the morning aid aircraft from Kismayo. When it landed, there was no sign of Seán or Mark. I was told that while they were travelling in the Juba Valley, figuring out whether the relocation programme could work, they'd been cut off by heavy floods. They had missed that plane and would arrive 'sometime'; no-one knew when. I soon realised that it was the aid worker's lot to expect the unexpected.

It was strange sitting there waiting for Seán at the airfield I had known before as a young RAF serviceman of 18. How things had changed. Nairobi West Airport, as it was then, had been used as a private flying club for the whites, with the odd private aircraft dropping in for an exclusive elephant shoot safari. Now it had moved on. I sat in the sun, waiting for Seán and Mark as each aircraft swung around in front of me and off-loaded its passengers.

They turned up only eight hours late, tired but fired up. The next day Seán and I flew to Mombasa where Seán fixed up an air drop supplying food to the starving in the Juba Valley. Then we had half a day together on the beach at the Two Fishes Hotel in Mombasa. Seán and I talked at length about Somalia and ran together along the same stretch of sand I had run on many years before. It was a good feeling watching his powerful shoulders in front of me. I had run here as a young man. How strange it was, I thought, that I was back 27 years later with a man who was my son. He joked about my inability to keep up with him: 'Better get rid of the cobwebs, Dad, if we're going to get beyond the trot stage,' he said.

It wasn't long before we were joined by tall willowy African boys, eager to keep pace with us and compete with the determination of a runner like Kenko. The intensity of the challenge was soon dispelled by Seán, who went through a variety of acrobatic manoeuvres, cartwheels and forward rolls, zig-zagging between his unsuspecting rivals and finishing off with a sprint that raised cheers and roars from the other beach runners which, I reckoned, could be heard in Nairobi. The race ended in one massive pile-up in the waves that engulfed the spirited youngsters as they collapsed in bursts of laughter.

When the run was over we sat drinking Tusker beer in the Two Fishes bar and talked about home. It was approaching evening and time for me to depart for London. Seán quickly wrote an account of the situation in Somalia. 'This is an important letter, Dad,' he said. 'People need to know what's going on. Please pass this on to Father Grogan at the Salesians in Stockport. He'll know what to do with it. I can rely on him to make sure it will go to the right people. I also want to make sure it's distributed to the various groups who've been supporting me in both Liberia and Somalia. And,' he added, 'there's a lot you can do, Dad.'

The letter was written in long hand, right off the top of his head, on the back of a Two Fishes menu card. The words of his letter impact on me more and more as each day passes.

He wrote:

'Greetings to the Parishioners of St Swithun's, Yateley and to all my friends in the Salesian Provinces of England and Ireland. A few words to keep in touch on how your kind donations are utilised here in the "Horn of Africa". I have heard some refer to Somalia as the "Hell of Africa". I suppose a fair comment, but not entirely true. I took up a UNICEF posting here in September after concluding my time with the Salesians and the UN in Liberia. It seems that I have gone from the frying pan into the fire, but I also like to think of it as an enriching, broadening experience.

'No doubt you have been exposed to the horror pictures of starving children. Sadly, it is a reality that has been brought about by man's greed

13

and not by natural disaster. There is no real drought in Somalia. It is a country which, prior to the war, exported rice and sugar in abundance; nomads wandered peacefully with their camels, goats and cattle, living a relatively healthy life. Everything was then turned upside down because of the greed and ego of certain men. Siad Barre, the former dictator, General Aideed, Morgan and Ali Mahadi, the so-called warlords, are the usual names mentioned in this battle of power. But one must add to the list the US Congress, the former Soviet Politburo, the Italian and British parliaments, apparently a noble collection of men and women who, over the years, approved the production and delivery of weapons of destruction to Somalia – for their own self-interest, of course. The greed starts here.

'Today in Somalia, in the southern part of Kismayo, I cannot walk from my house to my office (a distance of 400 metres) without heavily armed bodyguards. Thousands upon thousands of men in Somalia have their own weapons...they tell me this is for "survival". Boys of 14 live out their Rambo fantasies, believing they are fighting for freedom. They are so blind...but who can blame children? In Kismayo I wander through the market, checking the prices of looted UN food – wheat, rice, beans etc – and I see next to the bananas and camel meat AK47s, Kalashnikovs, Berrettas, M16s, Bazookas, varying in price from \$75 up to \$200 – all made in the so-called civilized world.

'Next door to my home is a shack with the sign "Spare Parts". Sadly, it's not for cars but for weapons, again made in the "civilized" world. We have a lot to answer for and you at home can do something by lobbying your MPs.

'The relief work here is extreme in all senses. The needs are massive, but the obstacles are also enormous. Normally, the UN, ICRC [International Red Cross] and other NGOs [Non-Governmental Organisations] have certain ground rules before they start to work, such as reasonable security on the ground, their own flagged vehicles that do not carry guns and the freedom to move and work independently to bring assistance to a people that they decide are in need. Somalia is regrettably the exception.

'UNICEF, like every other relief group, are forced to hire gunmen to protect their offices and houses. We hire looted cars that are escorted by armed men in order to move around. We pay through the nose at every stage to bring the donated relief items to the needy: at the port and the airport, for docking and landing fees, to porters to off-load the goods, to truckers to transfer the goods to the warehouses and distribution centres. But sadly, in many cases the beneficiaries are the market men and the various militias, not the innocent women, children and farmers who are most in need.

'The gun dictates everything here, and the biggest gun has the most power – Somalia now is simply lawless. The relief agencies, whose mandate is to reach the dying no matter what, acknowledge that we are subject to blackmail and extortion. But perhaps in some ways, by accepting this, we are perpetuating the conflict by providing finance for each gunman to buy more bullets which end up killing more people. The authorities, which vary from place to place depending on which clan is in power, seek to involve themselves in our work but only to squeeze out of us every penny that we have. Essentially they are the black Mafioso. Perhaps we have got everything wrong then. Maybe we should all pull out until the Somalis with the guns allow us to work freely. What if they say no? Perhaps the UN should send in 20 000 no-nonsense troops, ignoring the warlords' objections, and impose a safety chain for the secure delivery of the relief supplies. Perhaps we should ignore the warlords' arguments that we are imposing on their sovereignty. They know as well as we do that the country and its society have degenerated and factionalised to such a base level that arguments of sovereignty and self-dignity are now simply rubbish. I know from talking to the average Somali citizen that they are crying out for the UN to take over.

'The reality is that the various relief groups stay and struggle with the harassment and intimidation because innocent children are dying of starvation NOW – and their presence does make a difference... UNICEF are involved in special intensive feeding and health care for the severely malnourished, and our supplies brought in by German and Canadian Air Force Hercules planes are generally well-secured. We tend to succeed in getting this relief through to the children. Thankfully, feeding centres are now full of healthy and noisy kids. The general food distribution by ship, however, is less successful. In our last consignment of 3000 tons of wheat to Kismayo less than 30 per cent reached the target groups. We paid $160 000 to trucking contractors, all armed militias of course, to transport the food, with elders from the various villages and towns, who were supposed to escort the items. The food in most cases did not arrive, either because the elders made a deal with the truckers to divert the food to the market, or because it was intercepted by a group of bandits with bigger guns. The one good thing is that the looted food floods the market and the prices drop incredibly; now one bag of wheat (50kg) is worth 6000 Somali shillings – about 1 US dollar – a price that many can afford, but still there are many with nothing.

'In Kismayo today we have 50 000 displaced people, mainly farming families living in camps on the periphery of the town. They receive a cooked meal every day from ICRC (a dry ration would only be looted).

15

Now our aim is to resettle them back to their farms along a very fertile river valley – only 150 kms away – instead of reinforcing their dependence upon us and allowing this pathetic waste of manpower. UNICEF hopes to provide transport back to their homes with a resettlement package of food for two months, seeds for one year, materials to rebuild their homes, tools to farm their land and trained community health workers to ensure the appropriate distribution of UNICEF's drugs. By the next planting season, April 1993, we hope the displaced camps of Kismayo will have disappeared. But so much depends on security. These people will not move back to areas where there is fighting. The various clans must first agree to stop fighting. TIME WILL TELL.

'Life for myself is very up and down. I get so frustrated and fed-up when I have to deal with the authorities, the guards and the contractors. Their greed is sickening. In contrast I get such a lift when I get a chance to move out into the field and see how the feeding centres and health posts are running, and to regain contact with the more gentle face of humanity. Last week we cleaned the excrement and the mortars off the town's football field and had a soccer and athletics tournament for the kids of the displaced camps. The Somalis can really run...one clocked 12.5 secs for 100m. Compared to the Liberians they were useless at soccer. Salesian school, Chertsey U12 team would have beaten their "big lads" with ease!

'Next to the football pitch is an open field with hundreds of earth mounds. These are the graves of children who died six months ago. The contrast is so stark – but as I watched the energy and laughter of the children as they kicked the ball it brought home to me the message that where there is life there is always hope.'

Hope. For Seán it had been the foundation of everything he did, but it was a word that felt alien to me now.

We had arrived at the gate of the UNICEF Compound. A number of aid workers and Somali friends had gathered there to have lunch with us. We were greeted by Johan Svenssen, Seán's old colleague who had now taken over as Officer-in-Charge. Johan had worked with Seán during his first months in Somalia. He spoke fluent Somali and understood the culture well. Fifteen Belgian UN troops surrounded the UNICEF building, eight of them positioned on the porch. I was glad of their presence, though they should have been there from day one of UNICEF's arrival in Kismayo.

Bill and Mark discreetly led everyone inside while four UN troops escorted me to the spot where Seán was shot down. It was 15 yards from the compound gates – a dusty road with the desert sand banking up on either side. A crumbling wall stood on the right.

Mark walked to the exact spot. 'It was here,' he said. Unable to say any more he moved towards the wall, stood there and faced inwards. Bill surveyed the area, instructing two of the troops to position in the middle of the road, ten yards downwind from me. A small barefooted boy appeared from nowhere, stood alongside me and looked quizzically at my face. One of the soldiers attempted to move him on, but I beckoned him to let him stay. The boy smiled triumphantly. A sharp pain of anguish consumed my body. So this was the spot: the place where a bullet had struck Seán down. It now pierced my heart. I felt the pain that had afflicted Maureen, Theresa and Tania at home so suddenly, and their anxiety now that I too should be in this dangerous place.

I bent to pick up a stick, drew a cross in the sand and walked away.

Mark's hand was on my shoulder now.

We walked back to the gate in silence.

Back in the compound Seán's friends and fellow aid workers were joined by the Sultan and his dark-clad companion. The Sultan had befriended Seán and Caroline and they had often taken refuge in his nearby house when gunmen had come into the UNICEF compound in search of the aid workers and their money.

The Sultan spoke reasonable English. He talked about Seán warmly, admired his courage, regretted his tragic end, lamented the terrible loss to the Somali people and thanked me for his generous life. He said he appreciated all Seán had done for his suffering people and that Seán's name would always be remembered in Kismayo. His companion said nothing. His eyes were unfriendly and piercing. He was like a spectre as he sat there chewing qat – green plant leaves which, if eaten fresh, have the same effect as amphetamines. Qat was Somalia's favourite drug and was flown in every day from Kenya.

He spat out a black gobbet through his brown-stained teeth. I felt uneasy in his presence. I didn't trust him.

Many of the aid workers were now back in the building, including the two Somali national UNICEF workers, Ahmed and Farah, who had been walking with Seán when he was shot down. Johan, a quiet, reflective man who had been working with the Swedish Church before being seconded to UNICEF, had arranged a good lunch of local food. Although there was plenty to eat, I didn't have an appetite. As I sat at the table looking at the Sultan, his qat-chewing shadow, the mixture of faces and different cultures, the paid gunmen at the gate, I wondered yet again how Seán had come to be killed and asked myself if there was a Judas somewhere in our midst...
It was an ugly thought, but one I couldn't expel from my mind.

THE MASQUERADE

Now it was time for me to meet the UN Belgian Force Commander in Kismayo. The Belgian UN headquarters were based at Kismayo port, some distance away from the UNICEF compound. Once a busy trading centre, the port had recently been the scene of ruthless killings, harassment, exploitation and looting of the aid relief ships. It was quiet now, apart from the movement of the UN troops. The Belgian Force Commander occupied the building which had previously served as the Customs House before the civil war.

He turned out to be a rugged, no-nonsense military man, seated in his makeshift office. 'Take a seat,' he said. 'What can I do for you, Mr Devereux?'

I looked at him and thought, 'Is he living in the same world as me?' Anger welled up inside me.

'What do you think you can do for me, General? My son is dead, shot down by an assassin's bullet, while you and your men were here to protect him and his fellow aid workers. His killer is still as free as a bird with his two fingers in the air. I tell you what you can do for me, General, you can move your backside and get your men to track him down and bring him in.'

But the General was a seasoned veteran and had been on the receiving end of such outbursts before. 'I understand why you are angry,' he said. 'Seán was a good man, we know about him and the work he was doing here. We have some idea of the whereabouts of the gunman, but it's not easy to track him down. It's difficult to know who we are dealing with here, the clan element is strong. It's also ruthless. No one will talk. Life is cheap; if you want to live you say nothing.' His thick guttural Belgian accent gave his words greater meaning.

'There is no law and order in this country, we have no specific instructions as to what to do with him once he is arrested. Admiral Howe will advise you on this matter. Meanwhile we will do all we can. We feel bad about it too,' he said.

Our meeting was brief, to the point but somehow pointless. The General regretted the loss of such a fine man and promised to do all he could, once he was given a directive.

His senior officer escorted me to the waiting chopper and said that the pilot was available to take me to the Juba Valley and the memorial bridge named after Seán. During the 30-minute journey, we flew over small groups of settlements, a bombed-out sugar factory and farmlands. Every building was a ruin. Not a single matchstick remained in any of the dwellings. Roof-tops had been ripped off and even the shells of the buildings had been damaged by heavy fire. The pilot banked sharply to allow me a good view of the bridge, now spanning the stretch of water below. We put down in a field close by.

A small group of Somalis were waiting on the other side. Written on a large sign at the foot of the bridge was 'The Seán Devereux Bridge'. The US Marines had made a good job of erecting it, welding every single blot into place in case any were ripped out and sold for scrap. I crossed the bridge to greet the waiting crowd. Their colourful garments contrasted sharply with the grey steel of the bridge. Long-necked camels stood proudly above their owners, their pungent smell permeating the warm evening breeze. It was a biblical scene, caught in a time warp: the camels and their owners set against the might of 20th century technology mushrooming out of the wastelands of this barren place, the persecuted moving towards me to pay homage to a slain warrior. Seán would be glad that the bridge was now in place, enabling these farmers and herdsmen to move unimpeded through the valley for the first time. But for me and my family, how could it ever dispel our sense of loss?

I spent the flight to Mogadishu talking to Scott Peterson and Ann Wright. Scott was outraged and anguished by Seán's death. He had been in contact with Seán until quite recently. We talked at length about the media coverage of the Kismayo massacre on 13 December 1992, and of how the press had intercepted Seán when he landed in Mogadishu shortly afterwards. We spoke of his clear voice and his courageous account of what had happened.

The media circus had assembled in Mogadishu to cover the landing of 30 000 American troops on 9 December 1992; the UN's decision to deploy all 30 000 men into one area, leaving key positions such as Kismayo, Baidoa and Basseso unprotected, defied all logic, revealing the lack of clear-sighted military thinking which characterised Operation Restore Hope. There was no carefully conceived strategic plan to effect simultaneous deployment, no understanding of their adversary. In the event this weakness was quickly seized upon by the Kismayo warlord Omar Jess. While the military might of the American force sat in

Mogadishu contemplating its next move, Omar Jess and his ruthless gunmen went on a killing spree.

Seán had foreseen what would happen. He had feared there would be a massacre and was so concerned that he and Johan flew to Mogadishu immediately after the Americans landed on 9 December, to visit the American General Lawson W Magruder III. Seán pleaded with Magruder for the immediate deployment of troops into Kismayo. As he told the BBC: 'The people are crying out for protection. They will be happy even if the Martians come.'

But the might of the United Nations military machine moved too slowly. Seán and Johan returned to Kismayo and exactly what they had dreaded took place. Shots and screams rang out all night. By morning, around 90 people had been murdered. Seán and the UNICEF team brought in some of the bodies. The massacre caused a full-scale evacuation of international aid workers from Kismayo, but Seán and Johan were left behind because UNICEF owed $30 000 to local security staff, who were little better than gunmen.

Eventually, when Seán and Johan did manage to flee Kismayo for Mogadishu, they were met by a horde of the world's media who wanted to know the truth about the rumoured massacre.

Seán's dilemma was cruel. He could confirm the massacre and risk the consequences. Or he could say nothing and turn a blind eye to murder, and the UN's failure to deploy immediately in Kismayo. He was extremely careful not to pin the blame on any one particular warlord – in particular, Omar Jess – or ethnic group, but he could not deny the massacre. Some might argue that his decision to confirm the massacre was reckless. But if he had kept silent then the killing would have continued and the UN would have been let off the hook. Once the world knew of the massacre, then the UN troops would have no excuse. They would have to go into Kismayo. It was Seán's testimony that forced the issue.

Seán told the BBC: 'The whole night was filled with shooting and shelling and tribal killings. We believe about 90 people were picked out of their homes and killed. There was torture as well. There were targeted killings, a kind of ethnic cleansing if you like, in their last attempt before the troops came in.'

But a high price would have to be paid for such a courageous stand. It was exacted within days. The media were stunned and repulsed at Seán's murder. They identified with the principles for which he died and were determined that his voice would not be silenced. His words would survive him.

It was an article by Richard Ritenzburg of *The Washington Post* that led me to undertake this journey to Somalia in search of justice. Ritenzburg had written an account of the military investigation into Seán's assassination, an inquiry culminating in a report dated 27 January 1993, which gave the name of his killer as Abdi Dhere. I had tried again and again to find out the identity of the gunman from official channels, and what follow-up action had been implemented. I had tried to get hold of it through UNICEF, the US State Department and the British Foreign Office. So I felt angry and bitter that the first time we knew the name of Seán's suspected killer was from a newspaper article published in April, some three months after the report had been compiled. It was another lesson in the masquerade.

We touched down in Mogadishu – nicknamed Mog for short – in darkness. The aircraft came to an abrupt halt and the doors opened within seconds. A hot blast of air blinded our vision as we disembarked at speed. The airfield was a blur, American accents shouting commands: 'Keep moving, keep moving', 'This way, ma'am, keep moving.' A rugged Marine urged Ann Wright forward as she paused to check her handbag. 'Keep movin' ma'am, got to get you out of here, ma'am. This place is a hot potato, ma'am.'

We were bundled into a waiting jeep by four armed Marines. The jeep shot forward, jerking us back into the seat as the driver pinned the accelerator to the floorboards. Two armed escort vehicles on either side attempted to keep up as we left a cloud of sand in our wake. Twenty minutes later we burst through the UNICEF Headquarters to relative safety. Mark had assembled his staff and fellow aid workers for a special briefing to mark my arrival. I was glad to see among the group the friendly face of Father Jack Finucan, Director of Concern, the Irish aid organisation. Jack had attended Seán's funeral and concelebrated the mass with some 30 other priests. There were other familiar faces, but I could not recall their names.

The courtyard was fitted with a few benches and long trestle tables containing plates of local food, rice and water. The kerosene lamps flickered, catching the eyes of anxious faces in the crowd. Mark introduced me and invited me to speak. Unsure of what to say, I attempted a few optimistic lines. I spoke of Seán's commitment to his work, of his optimism for the future, the regret he would have felt at not being able to finish the work he had started. He would have hoped they would continue with the task, that a better future lay ahead. He would have been certain that some good would come of the conflict. And I knew he would want me to seek justice, not for revenge but as a moral obligation to all those who continue in the front line of humanitarian relief. Allowing Seán's killer to roam free would confer greater power upon him, thus allowing him to become tomorrow's warlord.

My words faltered, then dried up. Unable to continue, I looked at the sea of silent faces gazing at me across the flickering kerosene lamps, and sat down. Their glazed eyes conveyed a thousand messages. Suddenly, the silence was broken by the cry of a Somali woman as she raised her hands to her face, clutching her prayer beads and uttering words I couldn't understand. My own anguish was heightened, knowing that she and all the others were feeling the pain that had so brutally overtaken all of us at home. Gerry McCrudden stood up and lightened the tense moment: 'I think you could do with a stiff drink. Let's walk over to Rafferty's Only Wish It Could Be Bar.'

The phantom bar was a makeshift affair in a hexagon-shaped room. A collection of beer handles adorned the bar top: Guinness, Skol, Whitbread's, Yorkshire Bitter. Sadly, the liquid which flowed from the barrels below was Coke, Pepsi and orange juice. Memorabilia from various pubs around the world hung around the bar. The walls were covered with press cuttings and photographs of Seán. I gazed at them in disbelief, unable to accept the reality of what I was seeing with my own eyes: a kind of shrine to my son. His laughing eyes gazed at me, his voice ricocheting off the wall: 'It's only a joke, Dad. I'm right here, hiding behind the bar.' I expected him to pop up at any second, longed for this to be just another of his outrageous stunts. My eyes shifted to another picture. He was looking at me with that knowing smile. 'Yes, I have gone, Dad, but it's OK. You and Mom will be OK too, Theresa and Tania will be fine.'

The montage on the wall started to blur over as my legs weakened and the room began to revolve The voice of a man behind the bar brought me back to reality. 'We've been bloody depressed for the past few months,' he said. 'It means a lot to us that you've come here. If it's OK with you, I'll take these pictures down now. Like you said, Seán would want us to get on with the job.'

As accommodation was very limited in the compound, Gerry and I shared the room normally occupied by the UNICEF Press Officer, Ian McLeod, who was out of Mogadishu at the time. Ian had attended Seán's funeral in England and had spoken of Seán's energy, marvelling at his ability to pack everything into one day. Ian had reminded me that he too often ran with his father, and recalled how Seán's evenings rarely ended without a mini-marathon around the UNICEF Compound, usually about 15 laps.

Ian's room was equipped with a short-wave radio set and complicated communications system. From time to time the consort would burst into life. 'Are you reading me, over?' A litany of call signs crackled amidst American voices: 'Juliet-Bravo – Louisiana-Kilo-Delta, are you reading me? Come in, Tennessee-Bell! Roger over! Go-ahead, Affirmative! Over and out!'

The room served as a communications centre, administration office, exercise room and general store. Ian's racing cycle hung on the wall, his running shoes, tennis racket and other junk were piled up in the corner. The temperature was in the high 90s and the heavy, lifeless air oppressed me further; mosquitoes with their menacing spitfire-like sound bombarded my ears and neck.

Gerry was good company, easy to be with, a man of comfortable disposition. He had been in the Diplomatic Service for many years and was no stranger to remote parts of the world. A most unlikely First Secretary, he was small in stature but large in spirit. We talked about our earlier days in Ireland and laughed about the old times. Gerry was an accomplished writer with something of the theatrical about him. He was in the process of directing a performance of 'Dancing with Lunacy' at the Nairobi Theatre, which seemed rather appropriate in the circumstances.

Gerry's light-hearted manner helped to sustain me through those difficult moments, and he diverted my thoughts with his continuous rhetoric. Eventually tiredness overtook him as he slid off into a deep sleep. His last words were, if my memory is correct, a forlorn cry: 'Oh God, I would give a ransom for an iced gin and tonic.' I smiled at the thought of it as I lay there in a pool of perspiration, watching the bicycle hanging on the wall, illuminated from time to time by a passing searchlight from outside. I thought of Ian McLeod and his father running together and the years that lay ahead of them. The reality of never being able to run again with Seán was almost unbearable. Could it be that he would never move again? Salty tears mingled with my sweat.

Sleep was sporadic, interrupted by haunting dreams. Anguish kept forcing me bolt upright in my bed throughout the night. I lay awake, waiting for the customary dawn call of the muezzin to summon the faithful to prayer. But the nearby mosque was silent, the ancient ritual disrupted by the futility of war. How could it be that these faithful Muslims were killing each other?

My thoughts turned to the rest of the world and other raging conflicts: Liberia, Bosnia, Afghanistan, Indonesia and Ireland on our own doorstep. All in the name of so-called religion. But war was a million miles from any religion. Seán was right: it was about greed and we in the supposedly civilized world were fanning the flames of conflict by providing the weapons. Could we now feel proud of our role as peace-keepers, or were we simply easing our collective conscience by injecting aid workers and humanitarian relief into countries whose violence we had helped to perpetuate? We had a lot to answer for.

I slipped in and out of sleep for the rest of the night until dawn broke. We arrived at Admiral Howe's headquarters at 07 15. The UN HQ was based in old government buildings, with open-sided verandahs overlooking Moorish arches. But now this agreeable architecture had been transformed into a military fortress where security was rigidly enforced. Our vehicle was flagged down as we approached the entrance. The reinforced barriers were manned by armed personnel on either side. The officer on duty approached the vehicle, recognised Ann Wright, Bill, Mark and Gerry, but enquired as to my identity. On hearing my name he took two paces back, saluted and shouted a command to the Guard detachment to 'present arms'. The driver eased the car forward. Gerry said with a wry smile, 'I think they were expecting you.' The masquerade continued as a sergeant put large groups of soldiers through their paces. What a bloody silly world, I thought.

Admiral Howe's office was at the end of a raised wooden slatted corridor. We were led into an airy ante-room which opened off the Admiral's office. Various maps and aerial pictures of Mogadishu hung from the wall; a large briefing map pinpointed key trouble spots. It was a hive of activity, with military personnel hurrying in and out, telephones ringing, sharp precise conversations ending as quickly as they started. Outside jet fighter aircraft screamed overhead and helicopters blew clouds of dust across the open windows as they lifted off a nearby pad. The Stars and Stripes hung in a corner of the room. Below was a sophisticated communications system, which appeared to be linked up to the entire world. Coded messages spluttered out from a high-tech machine. It looked as though they were preparing for World War Three.

Suddenly the Admiral appeared. To my surprise, he was a young-looking man in his late 40s, tall, slim with a warm, welcoming face, casually dressed in an open-neck shirt and trousers. Ignoring the others, he held out his hand to greet me.

'It's a great privilege to meet you, Mr Devereux. I can't tell you what all of us here feel about Seán's tragic death. He was a very exceptional person. We're devastated at the loss of such a fine man. He was truly courageous in every way. You know he was doing a remarkable job here. He was making the difference. You must be truly proud of him.'

'Thank you, Admiral,' I said, 'I'm glad to meet you too.' I was disarmed by the sincerity of his greeting. I had wanted to launch into an attack, to ask what was being done, but I found myself modifying my carefully prepared opening remarks. Determined, nonetheless, to make a forceful impact, I began:

'I might as well come straight to the point, Admiral. I want to make it abundantly clear why I am here. I need to know why Seán was assassinated despite the protection of the most sophisticated military force in the world.' I went on: 'He had spent the afternoon of that day at a meeting with General Magruder – how was it possible that with 30 000 men on the ground, no-one was around to provide him with an armed escort back to the UNICEF compound? Why were his driver and vehicle missing? Why did he have to walk the half mile? Could you explain why I have not been able to access the Military Investigation Report, the one that gave a detailed account of the killing? The first I heard about it was through *The Washington Post*. How come? Worse still, the report says the killer was a man called Abdi Dhere. Is he Seán's killer and if he is, then why haven't you brought him in?'

The Admiral listened intently. His reply was considered. 'I am a father too, Mr Devereux. I know what you're going through. The report was compiled and completed by the Military Task Force on 27 January 1993. I don't understand why it was not made available to you. I can only assume that the authorities never asked for it. I'm very sorry it has caused you additional distress,' he said.

'OK,' I replied, 'I appreciate you concern, but you do understand that I won't be leaving here until I see the report?'

'Of course,' the Admiral said. 'We'll see to it that you have a copy before you leave.' He turned to Ann Wright and instructed her to ensure I received everything I needed.

I returned to the main question of Seán's death. 'Can you please tell me, Admiral, what steps are now being taken to arrest the alleged gunman? Why is he still free?'

He looked at me earnestly. 'You know how difficult things are in Somalia, Mr Devereux. There is no sovereignty, no government, no law or order, no judiciary. It's a bad situation. However, our mandate is to "restore hope" and change all that. The difference this time is that we have the muscle to do the job. Everything we do here from now on will be predicated on bringing Seán's killer to justice. The Elders of this country will have to decide on what action is taken once he is arrested. The people here must take responsibility for their own justice system. Their future depends on it. I want you to know that arresting Seán's killer is a top priority for us. Our intelligence sources tell us that he is located somewhere in the Juba region. We've been shadowing his whereabouts for some time and I have agreement that we can cross the border into Kenya and Ethiopia if necessary. We are also bringing in a team of experts from Germany to assist us in setting up a complete new police force. It's vital we get things right from now on.'

I acknowledged the Admiral's explanation and re-emphasised my mission, though I recognized the difficult task that lay ahead of him. I asked that he be honest about the political implications and warned against action that would escalate the problems. Above all, I did not want to be party to a masquerade. The Admiral was quick to respond: 'Like I said before, we will do the job, we are here to see that justice is done. I have assigned one of my senior officers, Major Woodling, to ensure no stone is left unturned. He will brief you on the details. You'll simply have to leave it to us, Mr Devereux.'

Realising there was no further need for dialogue, I extended my hand in a farewell gesture. Gerry was now on his feet. He shook the Admiral's hand and added: 'Everything Mr Devereux has said is fully supported by the British Government. We'll do all we can to assist you in your endeavour. Should you consider it appropriate, we can make the services of Scotland Yard available. You know you have a direct line to the High Commissioner.'

'Thank you, gentlemen,' replied Howe. 'It has been a privilege meeting you, Mr Devereux. I wish it could have been in less tragic circumstances. You must be very proud of Seán.'

To this day, Abdi Dhere remains a free man.

A Mother's Memories:
Formative Years

S eán was our only son. His birth, like those of our other two children, brought us great joy. He was our second child, 18 months younger than Theresa and ten years older than Tania. Theresa and Seán grew up together, though not exactly like a pair of lambs. They had very contrasting personalities, and there was never a dull moment as they shared their childhood wonderland.

Seán was fun-loving, a born organiser and leader, always enjoyed good humour. He was single-minded, quite stubborn and very untidy. He was remarkably self-aware and observant at a very young age, and seemed to have gained the benefits of self-assurance without the negative aspects of arrogance. He always tackled obstacles with unwavering dedication and kept his goal in sight. Sport was his real passion.

In the early years he did not take school seriously. Seán was more interested in what was in his lunch box and the games he would play at break time than reading or maths. His early schooling took place at Our Lady's Primary School in Crowthorne, Berkshire. The teachers were 'the poor Clare nuns'. Parents and teachers worked harmoniously together, which produced quite a unique atmosphere. It was a home from home.

The Sisters made sure fathers as well as mothers played their part. One day Seán arrived home with a note declaring that he would be starting needlework classes and required 50p for the appropriate materials. The request provoked a lightning visit to the school by his father, who protested vigorously. The headmistress, Sister Josephine, pulled a master stroke by casually announcing that in the absence of a sports teacher, there was no alternative to needlework classes. However, she could be persuaded to allow one or two of the boys' fathers to take the sport sessions every Wednesday instead of needlework. Thereafter the Wednesday school lesson plan bore the names Dermot Devereux and Percy Carter. Seán was somewhat miffed that his father ran the sessions, claiming that Dermot didn't know when the ball was offside or the left wing from the right wing.

It was not long before Seán's natural ability on the sports field became apparent. Having a young sister was a great asset. Tania became a built-in sports partner. By the age of 18 months she was negotiating her first six-inch high jump with her four major competitors, our household cockerels. Seán had already skilfully trained them to leap a two-foot horizontal bar in pursuit of their reward, a piece of bread. Tania's early training paid off as sport became her life.

This is how she remembers her brother:

'I only knew Seán for 18 years. Being the baby of the family I idolised my older brother and sister. I tried to look like my sister, to the extent of copying her make-up at the age of six, but to no avail; and I aspired to being as sporty as my brother. Sport was the bond between Seán and me. He would spend endless hours in the garden teaching me how to spin a rugby ball, hit a half decent golf shot, hurdle the fence and high jump the bamboo stick – which incidentally was supporting Dad's runner beans!

Both Seán and I gained a lot from his nurturing my love of sport and he managed to turn the most boring chores into something challenging and exciting.

Seán was always an extrovert, and you always knew when he was around. I distinctly remember one occasion, Yeovil, 9 July, 1989 – my first English Schools' Athletics competition, and God was I nervous! To my family's surprise I had got through to the final of the junior sprint hurdles, and it was all very serious. I was escorted from my team stand to the registration pen. On arriving I was confronted with big signs stating 'no coaches beyond this point'. I had to have my spikes checked and was informed of the random drug testing. All this formality merely added to my anxiety. The competitors were escorted into the warm-up area; no one spoke except the one girl who was letting everyone know her 'PB' (personal best time), which was considerably faster than mine.

I sat down in the warm-up area, watching all my competitors psyching themselves up, doing very flash drills up and down the warm-up track. I didn't even have a proper warm-up routine. I felt totally and utterly petrified; for the first time in my life I was going to get beaten!

Little did I know that Seán had been watching me from behind a tree, and could see that the seriousness of the event was affecting me.

'Pssst, pssst!' This intruding noise brought me out of my thoughts.

'Tan-yah!' I recognised that Mickey-taking voice. When I looked to my left I couldn't believe what I was seeing. There, popping out from behind the tree, was a creature in a fuzzy blue wig, rosy red nose and exploding eyes. He started leaping up and down behind the barrier. I didn't know whether to laugh or cry: ten minutes before the biggest race of my life and Seán was pratting around in a ridiculous outfit, about to be removed from the area by an unamused official. To this day I don't know how he managed to get in, but the memory will live with me forever. I couldn't stop laughing to myself and all those feelings of nervousness went. I ran the best race of my life. For the first time ever, Seán told me how proud he was of his little sister, and I could tell he was really chuffed – it was only on very rare occasions that Seán would be emotional towards me.'

Our house was always open to friends, extended family and overseas visitors from different backgrounds. We enjoyed having these visitors, and appreciated the cultural differences. The children were also glad, since they provided a diversion from the mandatory homework.

One day a Benedictine monk, Father Roger from Peru, came to stay. He was a striking man, very tall with great presence, and had worked in South America for 27 years. We were all fascinated by this intriguing character and the many facets of his personality. His account of life in South America revealed a deep spiritual side, penetrating intellect and ability to communicate.

On the second evening of his stay, we allowed Seán and Theresa to stay up late and join us for the evening meal. Father Roger had been telling us stories about Peru and its street children, and as the meal drew to a close and the dinner plates were cleared, he removed the small left-over portions of chicken and rearranged them on his side plate. He invited our bemused children to eat these, as he explained that such a portion of food would feed a boy or girl in Peru for a day. The full implications of this lesson was to become a living reality for Seán 20 years later.

Such was the ease of Seán and Theresa's new-found friendship with Father Roger, they felt able to plan an unexpected visit to his bedroom at first light the next morning. Their plot was to jump on his bed and rouse him from his sleep, but to their disappointment, the well-disciplined monk had already risen a few hours earlier. An immediate search found him standing on his head against the lounge wall. Two small giggling faces peered into the monk's with the question: 'Why are you standing on your head?'

His response was spontaneous: 'Sometimes the world seems upside down. It's important to view it from this perspective from time to time. It also helps me to contemplate and say my prayers.' Uncontrolled laughter followed, with a vain attempt to dislodge the monk from the wall.

Fr Roger was no stranger to children. The day before he left he became aware that Seán had to give a special talk to his class and was apprehensive about it. After breakfast he stood Seán on a stool at the other end of the lounge and said, 'Seán, if you are going to public speak today, this is how you do it. Hold your head upright, project your voice to the back of the room and speak loud and clear to me.' They repeated the exercise several times until Seán had mastered the technique. Thereafter, Seán had no problem with public speaking.

Visits from such interesting people broadened our own and our children's outlook.

Seán always had the capacity to enjoy any occasion for what it was worth, even when he was being chastised. His busy mind often led to him neglecting his personal possessions. He frequently dumped his prize bicycle on the lawn to be rescued by his father and on one occasion, frustrated by Seán's careless attitude and in an attempt to instil some sense of responsibility, Dermot roused him from his bed, making him get up and put his bicycle in the garage. Not wanting to be outdone and to make the most of the moment, Seán in his sleepy state mounted the bike and rode round the garden, thoroughly enjoying the moonlight experience.

He usually managed to avoid punishment altogether by using his natural charm in very winning ways, and he turned this into a fine art. Whenever he was confronted with my displeasure, he would flee to the home of his friend Roberto Nolli, whose warm Italian parents, Guiseppi and Angelena, could be relied upon to pour oil over troubled waters and fortify him with Italian delights from their table.

Dermot's job with British Airways gave us the opportunity to travel extensively and learn more about other cultures. The children were exposed to a lot of poverty in underdeveloped countries, and the contrast with their own privileged lives was stark.

In 1976 we visited Singapore. The country had not undergone the transformations that we see today and poverty was rife. One evening when we went for a stroll, Seán and Theresa noticed a weather-beaten old lady. She was scantily clad and shielded only by an old straw hat as she worked her way along an open sewer by the seafront, hacking mussels from the side of a drain. Later we saw her on the roadside boiling her catch of the day for her evening meal.

As Seán got older, he became more aware that children in other countries did not enjoy the same comforts as he did. I remember him aged about twelve, on a holiday in Sri Lanka, playing left wing in a football match on the beach with some of the local children. He was mindful that his new companions had virtually no clothes and nothing much to eat or drink, which concerned him a lot. So he pre-arranged a time for the members of his team to assemble by the hotel wall overlooking the beach. With great skill he removed large pieces of chicken from the evening barbecue and lowered them over the wall to the children below. Then, at the end of the holiday, he handed over almost the entire contents of his suitcase.

I have another haunting memory of a holiday we spent in Nairobi. We were walking through the market and Seán, still a small boy, helped me to choose the makings of a necklace from a bowl of Somalia amber stones. Years later in December 1992, on what turned out to be our last holiday together, we returned to the marketplace in Nairobi. There he recalled the day we'd picked the Somalia stones together and ruefully said, 'I can get you plenty of these ambers now, Mom, at a fraction of the price. They're hanging in abundance between the Kalashnikovs and the bananas in the marketplace in Kismayo.'

The hand of destiny may or may not play its part in life's precarious pattern, but it was ironic that his life should have ended there.

Seán made friends very easily. He was a great mimic. Over the years we spent many hours laughing until our sides ached as he pinpointed people's idiosyncrasies and cleverly imitated them. As well as being a gifted mimic, he was also a dedicated magician and compulsive practical joker who often pushed my patience to the limits. But his sense of humour is what I remember most about him.

I frequently fell victim to his constant pranks. Once some guests were complimenting me on the success of my Pavlova cake, and had asked me for the recipe. As I was listing the ingredients – 4 eggs, 4oz of sugar etc – to my horror, Seán appeared with the Tesco packet he'd salvaged from the garden bin, gesticulating half an ounce of Mrs Tesco and an awful lot of supervision from Mr Tesco.

At every get-together the inevitable mini-golf challenge was on the agenda, and on one particular occasion, I was again the butt of Seán's wicked humour. 'Watch Mom's classic pitch,' he said as he placed a ball on the tee and then watched it explode on impact, covering me in a cloud of white powder as though I had been hit over the head with a bag of flour.

Birthdays and celebrations were occasions Seán treasured, and remained so throughout his life. Our apple trees were once transformed into orange trees when he threaded garlands of ripe oranges through the branches prior to the arrival of some overseas visitors. He always liked to get a party going, organized everybody to participate: he was a born leader, a gift I recognised quite early in his life.

At the age of ten Seán's primary education came to an end and for the first time in his life he faced a serious test of his academic ability: the 11-plus examination. His success secured him a place at the Salesian College,

31

Farnborough. This school seemed ideal for him, as it was good for sport and had a fine academic reputation. The students were encouraged to adopt a caring and compassionate approach to life, to develop at their own pace and think for themselves. Seán excelled in this environment, spent seven happy years there and became the school captain. He took the Salesian philosophy seriously. He was deeply impressed by the founder of the Order, St Don Bosco, an Italian born in Northern Italy in 1815. Bosco spent his life in the service of street children, establishing a movement towards social engagement and human advancement. He set up small schools and vocational training centres for hundreds of homeless and uneducated children. Today, all over the world, especially in developing countries, these schools are well established by Salesian brothers, priests and nuns.

It was when Seán left the free world of childhood and was finding his feet in the quicksands of adolescence that I noticed very special qualities developing. Like most teenage boys his interests grew in many directions. Though sports and athletics were his passion, he wanted to enjoy and experience many other aspects of life. He had a great interest in geography, particularly human geography and issues relating to developing countries.

During this period he formed strong views on many matters, including what sort of life he himself wanted to live. He had a youthful but nonetheless profound interest in politics, and steadily became more analytical about issues that concerned him. Apart from bilateral nuclear disarmament, he felt passionately about equality, minority groups, race problems and the Third World. He always corrected me when I referred to the Third World: 'Developing world, please.' If I didn't have an opinion he would say to me, 'You have no right to be neutral, Mom.'

Sometimes I saw him as a bit of a socialist or, maybe more accurately, a socialist capitalist. He thought people should make money but not hoard it; instead it should be shared and developed with those less fortunate. He aired his views in support of the Liberal Alliance and Social Democratic values in the 1979 General Election, and was not impressed with the then tough pro-nuclear measures and foreign policy. He followed politics very closely and often took me to task when I lacked political awareness.

Seán seemed unusually free of self-doubt and gave himself completely to whatever activity he was engaged in, especially if he was in charge. One of his shortcomings was a belief that he always knew best. 'Don't do it that way, do it like this,' he would say.

'There are many ways of doing things, Seán,' we would say, and these words were so often repeated and mimicked that they became a family catchphrase

32

He was only 17 years old when he went to Birmingham University, where he gained a joint honours degree in sports science and geography, followed by a Post Graduate Certificate in Education at Exeter University. I often heard him say that his university years were the greatest years of his life.

After university he worked as a physical education teacher in the Salesian School, Chertsey. He loved children and had a very natural way with them; he saw them as the future and as he got older he began to talk more and more about underprivileged children. Towards the end of his time at university he had mentioned working in underdeveloped countries, so it was no surprise to us when he made his decision to go to Africa. He was aware that the Salesians were established in the capital of Liberia, Monrovia, and also ran a school in the interior. Seán was especially interested in the bush school, located in the township of Tappita, a very rural part of Liberia some 200 miles north-east of Monrovia. It was at this school that he volunteered to spend two years.

Liberia was then quite a peaceful place, so we felt happy about his decision and regarded it as a broadening experience, assuming it was only going to be for a year or two. But it was soon very evident from his letters home that his commitment to the education and development of children in Tappita, and Liberia in general, would continue. I realised that it was his vocation in life. I prayed at times, albeit a selfish prayer, that he would use his gifts in a less isolated part of the world. I had hopes that he might develop his career in Europe, where we would see him more frequently.

Theresa, who probably knew Seán best of all, saw his work in Africa as a kind of destiny: she had a gut feeling that he would work in Africa, though she never really thought about it. She believed it was his vocation and fortunately for him he was free enough in himself to listen to it. He seemed to have a very clear idea of who he was and what his principles were. Even as a teenager, she recalls, he could stand apart from the crowd without losing popularity and stand up for his values without being labelled a creep by his peers.

Seán's trips home from Liberia were a cause for great celebration. He was usually accompanied by one or two other aid workers. It was remarkable how quickly he adapted once he was home. He loved visits to the theatre and the London shows, but shopping at Tesco topped the bill. He and his great friend Michael Emery would push their trolley up and down the aisle for hours, viewing the vast array of foodstuffs. The selection of dog and cat food and bottled water left them speechless. They themselves, of course, could never resist returning with armfuls of goodies. 'Oh how I'd love to take some of the Liberian kids around that store!' he once said wistfully when he came back from his shopping trip.

On these rare occasions we all made a special effort to be home. The house was full of cheer and activity. The doorbell would ring constantly. Friends and family and favourite aunties would arrive. Theresa and Tania were the first to be on the receiving end of Seán's banter. I remember when Theresa arrived one freezing November night, having hared down the M3 in her worn-out Citröen, Seán was in the kitchen engrossed in arranging a mountain of food.

As he sees Theresa his face lights up. He gives her a big hug followed by the predictable quip about her hairstyle – 'very spinsterish' – and then he says, 'You're late.'

Tania arrives from a day's shopping looking very up-to-date in clumping black platform shoes, baggy jeans and layered top. She is full of youth and zest. Seán eyes her suspiciously. He never could get used to the idea that his baby sister had grown up.

Suddenly there is a roar from the TV. Seán darts into the sitting room and stares transfixed at the screen. Manchester has scored against Juventus in the European Cup. Seán is jumping ecstatically. The bread knife he is still holding is dangerously close to the crystal lamp. Michael comes through into the kitchen, his huge 6-foot-4 frame almost filling the doorway. He is armed with best Australian red wine and champagne. He pops the cork and the atmosphere partifies.

It was always a great novelty having Michael stay with us. He and Seán were great fun to be with and a marvellous double act, always full of hilarious Liberian anecdotes and exaggerated Liberian handshakes. They shared each other's love of good wine, food and any excuse for a celebration. They would meet up with various friends from the aid organisations 'Concern' and 'Goal', and lightning visits to Ireland were also high on the agenda. There they would visit family and friends, and my childhood home in Adrigole, County Cork. Seán loved Ireland, the humour of the Irish people and the pub culture, where he immersed himself in 'the craic' – a mixture of the spirit of fun you feel after winning a football match and the hilarity of an Irish wedding. He was so proud to be part of it and visited frequently, sometimes just for a day. During his busy schedule he never failed to return to his old school in Farnborough, sharing his experiences with the students.

When Seán was asked how much of a culture shock it was to go to Africa and experience life there, he invariably replied that it was a great shock to the system but not nearly as much of a shock as he felt when he returned to England, with all its waste and materialism. Perhaps he had forgotten a lot about his previous life in England. On the other hand, every time he returned, driving home from the airport he'd always remark on our wonderful infrastructures and how lucky we were to live in such a place. With Seán, the final focus was always on the positive.

THERESA:
INTO AFRICA

'There was a time when meadow, grove and stream,
The earth and every common sight
To me did seem
Apparelled in celestial light
The glory and the freshness of a dream'
　　William Wordsworth 1770-1850. (Ode: *Intimations of Immortality*, 1507)

Seán's affinity with Africa probably started with the name of my parents' first house. They called it Malindi after the place where they'd spent their honeymoon. I remember clearly the wooden oval sign in the porch – Seán and myself looking up at it, admiring the twirling 'M' and thickly painted palm trees, unaware of its incongruity in a suburban street in Surrey.

There was an old Masai shield and sword in the garage. To our childhood eyes they were huge and fearsome – we were fascinated by the unusual earth-brown patterns and intrigued to learn that the colours were made from a mixture of blood and milk. My father had brought them from Kenya, where he had been on national service. He loved it there and related many stories to us, spiced with his usual colourful descriptions and penchant for artistic licence.

Probably as a result of these tales, too many Tarzan films and my own imagination, I saw my dad as some kind of Indiana Jones figure, crawling through the undergrowth, negotiating with tribal leaders, saving villages and being presented with Masai shields in grand ceremonies of thanks. I was very disappointed when I eventually realised he'd actually swapped it for a few shirts at a roadside cafe.

At Christmas 1971 we went on holiday to Malindi and both Seán and I fell in love with the place. It has changed somewhat now but then Malindi was a beautiful unspoilt corner of the world. Clear blue coral seas washed crescents of white sand and endlessly tall palm trees clumped around the small hotels dotted along the shore. We spent long lazy days swimming, playing and pottering about the water's edge collecting beautiful seashells. At night the moon's rays danced on the waves and the beaches came alive with crabs darting out of pinhead holes in their hunt for food. There were frightening moments too, however. I woke one night to see a huge black beetle on Seán's mosquito net, and we were paranoid about the scorpions that lived under our cottage and the sharks that circled the bay.

Seán was only six then but already demonstrating his organisational ability. One day in the pool he organised all the children at the hotel in a water polo competition. I was surprised and secretly quite proud that the older children didn't object – I had always understood there to be an unspoken age pecking order but the nine and ten-year-olds just did what Seán said. He didn't always have such success. Mum often recounts the story of when he was four and had just started primary school – she found him crying with frustration as he tried to organise his new classmates into a line of pairs to lead out of school. They weren't having any of it and were bashing him angrily with their satchels.

One highlight of the trip to Africa was the journey to Malindi from Nairobi. It would have been easier to fly but we didn't have the money and besides, Dad liked the adventure and Mum was a good sport. It was a ten-hour journey along a remote empty road: hot, dusty and uncomfortable, not helped by the fact that we were all crammed into an old yellow mini because that was all the rent-a-car company had left.

The trip was broken up by exciting incidents. When we stopped at one lodge for a drink, I was pulled rapidly away from my chair by an ashen-faced Masai waiter. A deadly poisonous green mamba snake was slowly working its way between the green and white plastic slats on my chair.

Further on down the road was blocked for a time by a herd of elephants. Their big ears flapped in the breeze, their trunks raised and huge heads waving nervously. It was scary for a small child but Seán was quite fearless and got out of the car with Mum and Dad to have a closer look.

We stopped again to talk to a group of Masai children playing at the side of the road. Seán was very at ease mingling freely with them – he didn't seem to notice their meagre, tattered clothing or the flies gathering in the corners of their dewy eyes.

How strange to think that, 21 years later, his life would become so inextricably linked to theirs.

DERMOT:
DESTINATION LIBERIA

When Seán left England in January 1989, destination Tappita in Liberia, he travelled in the footsteps of Graham Greene. The Roman Catholic author of *Journey Without Maps*, fascinated by the 'dangerous edge of things...the honest thief, the tender murderer, the superstitious atheist', had crossed the wild forests of the West African state in 1935 and visited Tappita, suffering from diarrhoea, stomach pains and countless tropical fevers en route. There, Greene found a small prison next to the bungalow where he stayed.

The prison was a small dark hut with tiny portholes for windows: 'Each porthole the size of a man's head represented a cell. The prisoners within, men and women, were tied by ropes to a stick which was laid crosswise against the porthole outside... [One] old prisoner was a halfwit; I saw one of the warders beating him with his club to make him move to the tin basin where he had to wash, but he didn't seem to feel the blows. Life to him was narrowed into a few very simple, very pale sensations: warmth on his mat in the sun and cold in his cell...'

Seán was to go to one better than Greene in search of the dangerous edge of things. He actually spent some time in a Liberian prison, but that adventure takes place later on in his story, after the civil war had broken out.

Half a century after Greene wrote about Liberia it was much the same; still a wild place, one where the traveller has to put up with great discomfort, demands for bribes and, in the swampy heat, terrible ravages of the stomach.

When Seán arrived in the spring of 1989, Liberia was enjoying its last days of peace before descending into a cruel and mindless three-way civil war. The country's name comes from the Latin 'liber', meaning 'free'. It was created for the freed slaves of America's Deep South in the early nineteenth century, but Liberia had never quite lived up to the Utopian ideals of its founders.

Seán had found a job as a teacher with the Salesian school mission in Tappita, a day's journey inland from Monrovia, the capital of Liberia. He wrote his first letter home from the Salesian mission in Monrovia, where he was staying while he waited to go inland to Tappita.

He had arrived safely with all his baggage intact, and managed to get through customs with the help of a guide who negotiated a $10 fee with him – it had not taken long for Seán to see that the country was really corrupt when it came to officials and government servants.

Every morning, he would go jogging along the beach for 40 minutes, and some of the sights on the beach took him by surprise, such as men and women having 'a major morning off-load' (that is, going to the toilet) in broad daylight.

He had also been to a football match, which amazed him. The football wasn't any different but watching the crowd was a real education. About a quarter of the people were there to sell something: peanuts, plantain, chips, water, sweets, crawfish, kebabs, shoeshine and so on. One little salesman was about three or four years old; Seán couldn't believe how streetwise and independent they were at such an early age.

One incident in particular had made him laugh. There was a palaver outside his house, and a man grasping a huge stick was yelling 'rogue', causing half the village to join in the chase to catch this rogue, who had obviously pinched something. The mission cook told Seán that if they caught the thief, he would either be hospitalised or dead. As Seán said, it was a pretty impressive neighbourhood watch scheme!

Seán found the climate 'really weird', continuously hot and humid, always very hazy, but not as oppressive as he had imagined. He felt conspicuously white and lamented that he was not tanning at all. Such was life. The people he found exceptionally friendly and laid back, though it was really difficult for him to understand them. 'They never finish the last part of their sentences,' he wrote. 'If you ask them how they are they say, "I'm trying..."'

According to *The Rough Guide to West Africa*, Liberian pidgin 'sounds like nothing you've ever heard before'. In one traveller's opinion, it is 'as if a punch-drunk Brando of On The Waterfront taught all to drop the final sounds of each word and slur the rest'.

A few days after writing his first letter, Seán travelled up to Tappita. There is really only one road from Monrovia to the hinterland. It passes the Bong Mountains to the west, goes through the towns of Gbarnga and Ganta, crosses the St John River, and then through the village of Gre, a few miles distant from Tappita. On that journey, Seán went through six road blocks and had a small car crash on the dirt road – by the standards of what he was to go through later, an uneventful trip. He described his first thoughts of Tappita to the family in a taped letter.

The town was really poor, like a cowboy town. It was like walking into dirt, said Seán; no grass around, lots of tin shacks. They called it

Tappita city but it was really only a village. Seán's first impression was 'My goodness, what have we got here?' But once he got out of Tappita, to where the mission centre was, the view was fantastic. A hill area had been cleared, the land was beautifully green and a Spanish-type church had been built on it. As he came into the so-called 'Don Bosco' campus, Seán saw the beautiful clinic run by the Consulata nuns. Then there was the church and up on a hill, the school. 'Now it's all cleared and it's really quite magical and picturesque,' he told us.

Seán found Liberia a very sexist society with the women doing all the work on the farm and being kept back. 'I suppose it's their culture,' he said, 'which brings me on to the whole idea of the Christian bit here, because I mean half of them are Muslim... They're very God-aware people. Christianity is growing but it's not that big. I would question strongly how necessary it will be...' Seán would find his own position on that as things went on, but it was not really his main concern. His job was to teach English, RE and do a little bit of casual teacher training and sports.

There were three or four American Peace Corps volunteers in town, and Seán found it quite valuable having contact with young, white western people. He hadn't thought it would bother him, but it undoubtedly did. 'I'm beginning to realise that I'm in a totally different place and that to adjust to a different environment with different people is ambitious,' he said.

It certainly was a different environment. The meat stalls in Tappita market probably shocked Seán. They sold everything: groundhogs, porcupines, hogs, wild bush animals, crocodiles, fish, crabs, termites and bats.

Seán became great friends with the characters at the Salesian Mission in Tappita. The school principal was Fr Larry Gilmore, 30, 'a quiet chap, who looks like a kind of Greenpeace/Save-the-Earth type, with a big ginger beard'. Later, when required by the UN to sign a life insurance policy, Seán gave over all his worldly wealth to Fr Larry, knowing that he would use the money to look after Liberia's children. Fr Larry's role was to look after the management of the school and run the educational programme, in charge of the ten teachers and 1000 students, ranging from six to 26 years old.

Tappita's parish priest was another American, 37-year-old Fr John Thompson, cheese to Fr Larry's chalk. Fr John was, in Seán's words, 'a hysterical (funny) American...really good company'. He wore cowboy boots under his cassock and although he could easily be mistaken for a Texas cowboy he was born in Panama, one of 12 children. He was a Liberia expert, having been in the country since 1980, and spoke several of the local dialects fluently. When Fr John went out to the villages around Tappita he always announced his arrival by calling out 'yoo hooo!'

The Mr Fix-It at Tappita was Brother Donald, a tough Scot in his 60s. He maintained the complex, running its complicated generator and electrical systems 200 miles from the nearest well-equipped hardware store. In fact the entire mission depended on his ingenuity. Four Italian nuns, Consulata Sisters, ran the health care clinic, while a further ten Ghanaian teachers served on the school staff.

A month after his arrival Seán wrote to an old friend from Birmingham University, sculptor Sarah Healey. He told her of both his excitement and unease at being in a small town in Africa, and made fun of the importance of his own role: 'In the health clinic...I pose in my white jacket and stethoscope, always consulting my tropical diseases lecture notes – ha, ha!'

Up the hill from the clinic was the high school, very basic but functional. There were 800 pupils, their ages ranging from six to 25. The school was a lot more organised than Seán had expected – even the sports were well-established – and in one way, he had been a bit disappointed by this. 'I guess it's the old ego problem,' he confessed, 'because I would have just loved to have been involved in something that went from nothing to something great. No doubt I'll find plenty of things to satisfy me...'

That turned out to be true. His next letter to Sarah, a month later, was more relaxed. Seán had got himself a haircut, which had left him looking like 'a deformed American Marine'. Everyone had told him to go to the nuns to get his hair cut, but 'culturally broadened mugs' had decided to support the local economy and visit Gbongayes Barber Shop in town. It was a mud hut run by the only man in town with a pair of scissors, outside of which was a wonderful sign saying 'Doctor of Hair'. He (and everyone else) was really flummoxed by the white man's hair, and passers-by kept popping in to give advice here and there. By the end Seán had an audience of about 20, but it was a case of too many cooks; his head looked like 'a coconut shell'. Seán was philosophical. 'As they say here, "What to do?"'

After Seán was killed, it was Sarah who carved his headstone.

In another letter to the family in England, Seán explained that he had found his own little house, a small cottage behind the church, which was much better than the previous one. He had an excellent shower and sink, 'the best view you could imagine', and he'd even decorated the interior with 'Michelangelo classics'. He described it as 'a quaint little dwelling, kind of Latin American, with beige walls and rustic shutter windows'. He had landscaped the ground around in the hope of producing a good lawn, where he planned to play croquet and golf; all, of course, 'in order to amuse the Whitemon'! Seán had even prepared a little nursery there, where he could plant some nice crispy vegetables like celery, carrots and parsnips. Would we please send him out some lettuce and tomato seeds? In addition to all this, he had set up the 'Tappita Meteorological Weather Station' – or, more accurately, he had stuck a rain gauge in the ground outside his house. He was keeping a record of all the rain that fell during the year. The wet season had really started now and the roads were getting steadily worse, with mud ponds already forming on the road to Ghanta. Seán was told that in the heart of the rainy season in August, Tappita could be cut off for about four weeks. 'All very exciting!' he wrote.

Inventive as ever, Seán had devised 'a totally unique wet weather suit' to see him through the wet season. 'If you saw me in it...you really would laugh,' he wrote. 'Yesterday, I was "jammed", as they say here, as it was raining and I had no cagoule or wet suit. So Mr Imagination here took his British Airways suit cover and cut four slits in the arm and leg positions. With that trendy designer diagonal full-length zip, it really did look quite the part. The kids said I looked like a turtle...'

All in all, Seán was very happy and content. He described his new cottage as 'too fine', a typical Liberian compliment. Kids would pop in and out all day because they saw it as 'Mr Seán's' house now, and they would sit and chat all day long if he allowed them to. 'I'm really beginning to get quite an insight as to how they live their lives,' he wrote. One boy, 'Saturday Frazer' and his brother 'Wisdom', both 16 and in Seán's class, had never been outside Tappita district. They had never even walked the other side of the Immigration Checkpoint. To Seán, it was mind-boggling.

An infection known as 'Apollo infection' had been going through the school, and Seán had contracted it. It was a form of conjunctivitis, where the whole eye swelled up. In his case it had lasted for a week; the sisters put him on some penicillin ointment straight away and that seemed to do the job. The locals called it Apollo because the infection first came to Tappita in 1967 during the time of the space mission to the moon. People associated the disease with looking into the sky, which at that time had contained the Apollo spacecraft. As Seán would discover, Liberians were very superstitious people.

Seán was only now beginning to realise the extent of the health problems in Tappita. 'It's true that the people are marvellously strong with an incredible immune system,' he wrote, 'but I'm told that 70 per cent of the population will have the malaria virus in them, with 20 per cent at any given time (that's 150 plus) actually suffering from the symptoms.' Many of the children had open sores and also rising pus-type boils. The thing that struck Seán most was that they made such little fuss; there was no whining or moaning or attention-seeking: 'If you're ill here, you just lay down!'

One of the things that Seán initially found hard to get used to was that the aid workers, priests and nuns had cooks – or, as they called them, 'houseboys' – who did all the cooking and cleaning. For Seán the idea, and especially the name, conjured up ideas of colonialism; but on the positive side it provided useful employment for the locals, so he eventually managed to come round to the idea, though not easily.

He raved about how good the food was – tons of rice and a thing that was like palm butter. The houseboys took the old palm kernels and bashed them to produce 'lovely pulpy stuff' which they then cooked and poured over the rice. They also chopped up potato greens and added rice. Meat was a bit of a problem, but the Salesians spent a lot of money on food, there was no holding back. Once when they killed a chicken, Seán had been a bit shocked to learn it was one of the chickens from their yard. He'd noticed there was one short after the meal and they all had a good laugh on him.

That morning they'd bought a leg of deer. A man was going through the forested area selling the odd leg of deer for £15, and a black, velvety, hairy leg appeared in the kitchen, ready to be skinned and cooked. Seán managed to eat it but it was another thing that would take some getting used to.

Seán's sister Theresa went out to Liberia to visit him later in 1989. He came down from Tappita to Monrovia and they went to the beach. One incident from that day sticks in Theresa's mind. On the beach Seán and his sister met an American working in security at the embassy. He invited them over for dinner. His house proved to be huge, surrounded by guards and wire. Four others were there and the evening appalled Seán because the guests were anti-Liberia and anti-Liberian. After dinner Seán and Theresa walked home, discussing the evening. Theresa recalls Seán saying: 'They make me sick the way they talk about black people. What are they doing in this country if they are so against it?'

On another day in Monrovia they went for a walk in town and suddenly there was a lot of noise and a real commotion. Seán cried out 'Stand back!' as a cavalcade of black limos surrounded by motorbikes with lights flashing and horns blaring passed them by. He turned to Theresa and said: 'That's Doe.' Doe was the current (and brutal) Liberian president. Chaos followed in the wake of his motorcade: carts turned over, fruit rolled over the road and someone fell off his bicycle. Seán and Theresa roared with laughter, but Seán went on to add: 'They just go straight through at 80 mph. Every now and then, someone gets killed.'

The journey to Tappita was a nightmare for Theresa, although Seán had hired a taxi as a treat. The taxi was jam-packed with humanity, but apparently the buses were worse: you could end up sharing your seat with a chicken or a pig. The road was a dirt track through the forest riddled with potholes, and logging lorries would come screeching down the road at high speed. The car broke down and suddenly all these Africans appeared out of the forest. While the car was being repaired, Theresa was surrounded by children and all she could think of to entertain them was her make-up bag. They were fascinated, particularly by her eyelash curler, and they played a game guessing what it was used for. They really chuckled when she showed them, and said, 'very kwi', which means 'very white'.

They got stopped at endless checkpoints and when Theresa asked Seán what they were for, he said: 'Oh, it's in case there's a revolt, as if there would be here. I mean, what a load of rubbish.'

They arrived at Tappita late in the evening; Fathers Larry and John and Brother Donald all rushed out to greet them. Theresa found all the team at Tappita delightful characters.

On the way up Theresa had been very careful about what she had eaten. She avoided nearly everything, but ended up eating ten oranges sold by people at the roadside. That night she was very ill and Sister Carmen, one of the nuns, looked after her. She stayed with the nuns in their house, which was very basic, just a bed, a mosquito net, chair and a cross on the wall.

Theresa visited the school, which was like three barns. The kids sang a welcome song to her and she played a game of rounders with them. At lunchtime, the priests would bring out a huge pot containing an oily pastry cake that was sprinkled with fish powder, rich in minerals. The kids would help themselves, eating with their hands. To the children of Tappita, the school lunch was not far off a banquet.

Theresa had at least one admirer, the Liberian cook, William. He had obviously taken a fancy to her during her visit because he wrote her a letter which Seán passed on during a later visit to Europe.

William wrote: 'I think you're the most beautiful, wonderful, fantastic woman that I've ever met and may God be with you... PS Could you please also bring a Walkman and TV set next time you come.'

Seán, roaring with laughter when he handed over the letter, said, 'Well, Theresa, it's worth a try...'

However, there was a dark side to life in Tappita. Theresa remembers that Seán got very upset when one of his pupils died as the result of an abortion. A girl had come and knocked on the nuns' door in the middle of the night, bleeding. Sister Carmen tried to help the girl but she died.

Theresa also picked up rumours about ritual killings. A year before a young child had been kidnapped, killed and her heart taken out and eaten to give power to the government. Seán told Theresa that it was best not to talk about such things.

But then, as later, he felt pain for those he could not help.

'How Dat Body Today, Man?'

Seán had been in Liberia about six months when I decided to visit him; we both enjoyed these father-son reunions. We had planned a four-day visit, most of which would be spent in Tappita. Seán was to coincide my visit with a trip to Monrovia in order to acquire the monthly supply of medicines, food and other equipment.

On my arrival at Monrovia's Robertsfield Airport I was met on the tarmac by a white-robed figure, Father Joe Brown, a Salesian priest. He had been in Liberia some 15 years and was well known. The Salesians had set up the Arthur Barclay Polytechnic Institute, which in the Liberians' eyes was a kind of Eton College through which many famous local politicians and prominent professionals had passed. Father Joe had clout.

It was common practice at the airport for corrupt officials to hassle an incoming passenger until a bribe was handed over. The officials were good at inventing some spurious reason for not allowing the individual to enter the country, such as: 'You have no letter of welcome'. But Father Joe was afforded diplomatic status which enabled me to avoid harassment by customs and passport officials.

The priest had mastered the local pidgin English. Fr Joe greeted all the officials by name and asked : 'How dat body today man?' It proved to be a winning formula.

We drove into town in the Salesian's well-worn vehicle on a disintegrating dirt road, steering carefully around the many water-filled potholes. Joe said that to 'splash someone here is as bad as running them over'.

The rising heat fused with the stink of bad drains, stagnant water and rotting garbage on the streets. My misguided belief was that the legacy of America's earlier involvement in the country would have been a well-ordered system, but the stench, rutted dirt road and the run-down shacks at the roadside soon killed off that notion. Yet the homes were colourful, painted vivid blues, pinks and greens, nearly all of them roofed with the poor man's slate – galvanised tin.

An array of hoardings proclaimed a multitude of religions, each with its distinctive slogan: 'Everlasting Love Winning Africa', 'Jesus Loves You', and, 'I am the way and the light'.

The Arthur Barclay Institute was a complete contrast from all that stood around it. Located at the not-so-lovely sounding Monrovian suburb of Sinkor, it stood out as efficient and well-run. It had well-equipped classrooms, complete with computers. The centre acted as a communications link between Tappita and the outside world. Routine contact was made twice daily. The early morning link had revealed that Seán was delayed and was now scheduled to arrive the next day. It appeared that their only serviceable vehicle had 'chronic engine trouble' so Seán would now arrive in the Primary Health Care ambulance, once it had returned to Tappita from upcountry.

With a day now in hand, Father Joe suggested a visit to Lake Piso situated some 75 miles north west of Monrovia. The lake was a bolthole for the priests who, on rare days, were able to retreat from the oppressive climate of Monrovia. An old motor boat complete with fishing tackle was housed near the lake and provided an opportunity for a day's fishing.

We departed late morning and drove through the city of Monrovia. Father Joe was anxious for me to see the sights, such as they were. We stopped at the Presidential Palace, the 'Mansion House', where President Samuel Doe was in residence. Joe gave me a potted history lesson on the development of the country and how each president had come to power down the ages. He ended by telling me how the heads of those on the wrong side in the last *coup d'état* had ended up on the flag poles outside the Mansion House: a grim reminder to others who might have similar intentions.

'It's a good job those dark days are well behind us,' I said.

'The dark days are still very much with us,' said Joe. 'This happened only four years ago. The pot's still boiling, ready to spill over at any time.'

President Doe himself had taken over the government after toppling William Tolbert in 1980. Tolbert was slashed and shot, his Cabinet executed on the beach in front of the TV cameras of a horrified and repulsed world. But, in truth, Doe's brutality was only more public than Tolbert's. The latter had run a cruel despotism. He was the last Americo-Liberian President, a descendent of the first settlers, repatriated American slaves who had founded the country in the 19th century. From the 1820s until Tolbert's death, the country suffered under a kind of apartheid, with the descendants of the freed slaves the ruling elite lording it over the indigenous Liberians.

Gun law was no stranger to Liberia. It was present at the birth of the country. Records show that in 1882, freed men set sail from the southern cotton plantations of the Deep South in small schooners. The return trip to Africa was sponsored by the American Colonisation Society, led by men like Henry Chay and Daniel Webster.

US Navy Captain Robert F Stockton accompanied the first black Pilgrim Fathers who put ashore on the spot which is now known as Monrovia. The event was supposed to herald the end of the slave trade. But the freed men needed land. The captain struck a deal with the local chiefs. They gave him the land to create Monrovia. In return, he handed over $300 worth of arms, including six muskets and a barrel of gunpowder, with a promise of 12 guns and more gunpowder to follow. The captain set a dreadful precedent.

The newly arrived settlers had high hopes. The constitution was drafted at the Law Schools of Harvard and Cornell Universities and first promulgated in 1847. When Liberia became a state, the national motto was 'The love of liberty brought us here'. Liberty may have been the big idea, but not for the indigenous people. The settlers set about exploiting the locals and enslaved them with a ruthlessness that could be compared with their own former masters'. The constitution read: 'We, the people of the Republic of Liberia, were originally the inhabitants of the United States of North America...' – a proclamation that took no account of the other 95 per cent of the population.

Liberia as a state was, in those days, not much more than a thin strip of land running 25 miles in from the coast. The interior was still an unknown place run by traditional chiefs. The Liberian Government in the last century was accused of hunting down the people from the interior and shipping them as slaves to the island of Fernando Po. It was a grim history lesson, which was soon to become yet grimmer. On the journey to the lake I experienced the underlying tension to which Joe had referred. We had to pass through a number of checkpoints, manned by President Doe's ragtag army, an undisciplined and aggressive group of thugs. We were flagged down at the first checkpoint by a large bull of a man. He was clearly set on giving us a hard time in order to extract a bribe. Father Joe leapt out of the vehicle.

'How dat body today, man?' he asked. The bully halted in his tracks as he recognised the white-robed figure.

'Oh, it's the faather. I am feeling faaine, Faather.' He extended his hand, gripping Joe in the traditional Liberian handshake: a grasping of the hand, followed by a clinching of the thumbs, then a clicking of the middle finger as the hands are withdrawn, a symbol that they are no longer slaves.

The custom, they say, dates back to the days when slaves in America had the top of their middle fingers cut off to show their enslavement.

'You going far da fishing, Faather?'

Joe said yes.

'Oh dat vaary vaary good, Faather! Who dat bossman with you, Faather?'

Joe responded with a gesture of the hand: 'Oh he just dat new faather coming far da visit!'

'Oh vaary vaary good, Faather. You batter keep gooin, Faather, if you gooin to caatch 'em today.'

The barrier went up as Bully Boy requested a double blessing. The priest raised his hand, administered the blessing and we were on our way again. A short distance beyond the checkpoint, Father Joe stopped the car and gave me a white cassock from the back seat.

'Put it on. It's your new uniform for the rest of the trip. You can give the next blessing,' he said, laughing loudly.

The lake was a vast expansive place, set on the edge of swamp lands. Beyond was the mouth of the Atlantic Ocean. The water was inviting after the long, hot and dusty journey and, at the risk of contacting some incurable water-borne disease, we plunged in. Refreshed, we took the covering off the boat in record time. The engine fired on the third attempt and we headed out into the lake. Father Joe did not delay in casting out the fishing lines as we entered quieter waters. The engine was set on idle, allowing the boat to gently ease forward, trawling the lines in its wake. It was supremely tranquil.

My thoughts turned to England and home. The green fields and hedgerows now seemed a long way off. I wondered how Seán had adjusted to the remoteness of this place and to what extent he would have changed.

After a successful and very memorable day's fishing, we headed back to the shore. A warm welcome awaited us at the Barclay Centre. The Liberian cook was overjoyed at the sight of the big fish we'd caught, which provided the evening meal, a handout for those in need and a small quantity to be consigned to the freezer for days to come.

The next morning I was woken up very early by the sound of an ambulance siren. That's him, I thought, Seán has arrived. We always knew when he was around. I launched into a pair of shorts and headed towards the siren. Seán was off-loading a number of empty containers with the help of eager street children he had picked up on the edge of town. He had nicknamed the youngest of the kids the 'Flying Doctor' and had instructed him to clear the streets by sounding the siren as they headed into town.

Seán looked fit and well and was clearly delighted that I had arrived. He greeted me, asking after everyone at home, and announced that we had plenty to do with a busy week ahead.

We did not delay more than a night stop at the Barclay Institute as the ambulance was needed up country for emergency use. Medical supplies were collected from the *Medicines Sans Frontières* base in Monrovia. The charity was a well-established aid organisation which worked closely with other NGOs (Non-Governmental Organisations) in Liberia.

Shopping was an education. Seán needed to buy virtually everything in Monrovia, goods we could find in any corner shop back home in England: tinned fruit, flour, rice, toiletries, paper, school equipment. He split the work with the oldest street boy who was still tagging on. Seán asked him to get hold of the perishables: fruit, vegetables, palm butter and so on. Seán had already agreed with the boy a local price for the items; it was down to the lad to use his street wisdom to find the best possible prices and make a few dollars for himself. During the shopping spree I suggested that we purchase two large sacks of potatoes from the supermarket. Seán, however, had decided to get them in small quantities from the old market women who lined the street by the store. He wanted to ensure that each one achieved a sale that day.

As we approached this large group of colourfully-dressed women, African reggae music bellowed from a shiny new ghetto blaster. The women swung to and fro to the rhythm of the music. The potato buying became something of a spectacle. Seán proceeded to purchase a small bag of spuds from each one. The women were not lacking in enterprise, adding a few Liberian dollars to the price of each bag. Seán playfully protested in his pidgin English, claiming he was not a tourist but a local man. To prove his point, he started to dance in rhythm with the reggae, engaging three of the older women in a traditional West African dance. Soon there was much hand-smacking and laughing. One delighted woman called out: 'Oh da white man, he can dance too faine.' The rest of the women joined in, followed by a small crowd in the street. A passer-by applauded and called out: 'He da only white man who can teach da African to dance.'

The remainder of the evening was spent with our friends at the Barclay Institute. We consumed a few crates of beer amidst riotous banter and good humour, but we were still awake at daybreak next morning, heading up country to Tappita. Seán briefed me that we would have to negotiate our way through 20 checkpoints en route to Tappita, a prospect I did not relish.

Tappita lies some 286 miles north east of Monrovia through remote open country. The monotony of our journey was broken by a number of townships, largest of which is Ghanta, 80 miles short of Tappita and famous for its leper colony. There, the tarmac road ends and the rest of the trip was undertaken on murrum road through the thick vegetation of the rain forest. The road is impassable during the rainy season and Tappita can be cut off for long periods. Fortunately it was the dry season during my visit.

The air was much lighter up country, the dry heat contrasting with the humidity of Monrovia. We expected to cover the journey in six hours. However, much would depend on the degree of harassment at the various checkpoints. Seán had considered this prospect and had developed a contingency plan. I was to be strapped in the ambulance bed and to assume the role of a seriously ill patient. Each barricade would be approached with blue emergency light flashing and sirens sounding full blast. The strategy worked well, for as we approached each checkpoint, we were flagged down by the guard who peered through the window of the ambulance. He heard the agonised groans of the sick man within.

'What wrong with da boss, man?' asked the guard.

Seán, hiding his laughter, replied: 'That fellow vaary vaary sick. We have to get him to da hospital too quick.' The barriers were lifted by the guard after a little hesitation but not before he had warned us that we would have to give him 'plenty good Sunday' next time. 'Sunday' is the pidgin term for backhander or handout. Our luck held out and, with the exception of a thorough search of the ambulance at two checkpoints, we made the journey in just over six hours.

On the outskirts of Tappita, Seán pointed out the home of the local witch doctor. She was hobbling outside her hut by the roadside, an eerie figure, old beyond her years, clad in garments of various colours. She moved in a trance around a collection of African pots, carvings, bones and voodoo fetishes. Her home, where she lived alone, was an oval-shaped mud hut with straw thatch. Seán said that from time to time they involved her in some healing process with patients at the clinic. There is a strong belief in witchcraft in Liberia which is deep-rooted and permeates the culture. Most Liberians live in fear of the voodoo. There are numerous bizarre juju rituals, many of which involve children. They became a devastating reality during the horrors of the civil war which erupted a year later.

The belief in sorcery did not confine itself to times of conflict. Even in peacetime this darker side of the national psyche belied the everyday gentility and religious devotion. Voodoo was exported with the slaves to the cotton plantations of America's Deep South where it was celebrated in the darkness of the night in secret ritual and used as a weapon of fear and despair. When the freed slaves came to Liberia, they were still manacled to the old voodoo practices. Freed men they might have been, but the spectre which haunted their souls lived on. Today in Liberia few are impervious to the supernatural.

Seán often spoke later of the frightening fetishism that gripped many of his young students when they became boy soldiers and rebel leaders. During the war ritual murders became commonplace, with the victims' body parts used in voodoo ceremonies. The heart and other vital organs, mixed with drained blood, provided the black magic which would protect the believer from evil. So strong was this belief that witch doctors claimed to have power to make their clients bullet-proof, spear-proof, knife-proof and fire-proof. President Samuel Doe himself laid claim to his immortality through 'proofing'. 'No bullet or knife can touch me,' he once boasted. He was to be proved wrong.

Equally unfortunate was the official whose death Seán had heard about. To test his own voodoo 'bullet-proofing', he shot himself at point blank range. He died minutes later. The rebel leader Charles Taylor also resorted to the service of a *marabout*, a type of Muslim seer or soothsayer, who wore protective charms around his neck. Of course, people wear charms back in Britain, but in Liberia such things can have a sinister side.

Tappita City had a population of some 8000 and was one of the main towns of Nimba County, the forested hinterland far from the capital. Several coup attempts against President Doe had been initiated from the Tappita district. As a result, the region was the last to benefit from government expenditure. Living standards were far below the poverty level. Most of the inhabitants were subsistence farmers. A few Lebanese businessmen ran most of the stores and were the mainstay of the economy. The township's homes were mainly constructed of wood and galvanised tin. To look at, the city was little more than a collection of mud huts sprawled out across the hillside.

The Salesians' compound was slightly out of the town on a hillside. The church of St Frances stood together with a number of school buildings, and, close by, a Primary Health Care Centre had been set up. The green playing fields, flowering bushes and mango trees surrounding the buildings contrasted sharply with the dilapidated state of the town. The complex provided stability and optimism for what was otherwise a struggling community. It was the result of a pioneering effort by the Salesians.

On arrival at the complex we were greeted by Fr Larry, the quiet American, Fr John, the no-so-quiet American, and Brother Donald.

Seán's accommodation was a makeshift outhouse attached to the back of the church. It comprised a bed, a mosquito net and a small table. He used his suitcase as a wardrobe. A small roll-up sleeping bag was positioned in the only other remaining space in the room which I was to occupy. It was late in the evening but a special meal had been prepared in my honour. It consisted of curious African dishes which required a strong constitution. Fortunately it was washed down with large quantities of beer that we had bought in Monrovia. The evening was alive with conversation, laughter, endless banter and the unfailing ability of Fr John to cap every story with a better one.

Midnight was quickly upon us. Seán reminded me that he had agreed to visit a sick boy on the edge of town with vital medicines he had acquired in Monrovia. Somewhat reluctantly, I said I would go with him. Our transport was a not-so-high powered Honda 175 motor cycle, a 'Hot Rod' specially tuned by Brother Donald. We sped into the night, zig-zagging across rough terrain. Screeches of laughter filled the air as Seán tried, unsuccessfully, to dislodge me from the pillion seat into the dusty road.

Dishevelled and a bit unsteady of foot, we approached the humble dwelling. In spite of the late hour, the boy's family were assembled around a small fire in front of the house. They had been waiting for Seán, certain he would come. I was touched by the warmth of their welcome and obvious regard for him.

'We are too glad to see you, Mr Seán. We know you come before morning time. We are 'appy you come, Mr Seán.'

'This is my O'Pa,' Seán said as he introduced me.

'Oh, this you O'Pa, Mr Seán. He look too much like you, Mr Seán. We are too 'appy to see him.'

I was immediately given the seat of honour now vacated by the elder of the family. This gesture was accompanied by the offering of a jug of milk and gruel. I sipped it slightly uneasily, I am ashamed to say. The elder, an old man of advanced years, beckoned me to be seated as he positioned himself next to me. His weathered, criss-cross-lined face shone in the light of the fire; his cheekbones were highlighted as he drew on his long clay pipe. He smiled approvingly as Seán attended to the sick boy and instructed the mother what to do with the medicines. The old man spoke of his many children and of happier days, when his people moved peacefully from one place to another. Now life was 'faster', many things were changing, the land was different and the people were different too. He had lived too long and was waiting for his time to go to a better place. I asked him if he was 80 yet. His response was not particularly enlightening: 'I was born in the rainy season,' he replied.

Talk of the rainy season was an ideal cue for one of Seán's tales. This one was about the time he went on a madcap journey to the leper colony near Ghanta. Seán had gone there on his motorbike, a distance of some 60 miles, to visit the colony and assess the needs of the 700 inhabitants. The colony had its own clinic, vocational area, recreation facility and shopping complex, and the Leprosarium was a model of cleanliness with its white-washed houses and neatly trained thatched roofs. Small white stones lined the driveway leading to the centre of the complex. Harmony and a sense of tranquillity prevailed amidst the afflicted.

It was the rainy season at the time of Seán's visit and the roads were virtually impassable, but somehow his gallant little motorbike stood up to the demands on its engine. The return journey at midnight was a different story, made hazardous by the moving mass of mud-flow from heavy rain and unfamiliar terrain. Then the headlamp failed and the clutch, which had been overheating, finally succumbed to the conditions. Not technically skilled, Seán was forced to push the motorbike in the general direction of Tappita.

The rain continued relentlessly in the blackness of the night. Soaked to the skin and apprehensive of the unfamiliar territory, Seán forced his way along a mud bank. The motorbike slid from side to side while he attempted to keep it upright and maintain his own balance. Inevitably, the machine disappeared into a large crater in the road, followed by Seán, who tumbled spreadeagled into a mud bath. He lay there exhausted, unable to move. The torrential rain showed no mercy as one massive mud-slick after another was washed off the road into the crater. The hole was filling up rapidly.

Suddenly, urgent, excited voices sounded and anxious hands pulled him to safety. They carried him to their nearby village, washed him with buckets of hot water, fed him flour-maze and hot milk, wrapped him mummy-like in sack cloth and watched over him as he slept in a makeshift hut. He awoke at daybreak to the sight of two small boys viewing him curiously. They ran to inform the elders that the 'kwi', the white man, was alive. He was offered food and fresh water together with his washed and dried clothing.

As Seán unwrapped himself from his mummy-style garment he saw dozens of mosquito bites. He had been badly bitten all over his body, having shared his accommodation with several hundred mosquitoes. As he rubbed himself, the hospitable villagers had been unable to comprehend that the 'kwi' did not have the same immunity as themselves. They offered a local herbal paste to ease the itching of the bites, then rescued the motorbike from the watery garage and loaded it on to a logging truck which they had halted on the road. They fed the truck driver and rewarded him with a sack of vegetables as payment for the delivery of the 'kwi' to his destination at St Francis, Tappita.

Ten days later, the exact incubation period, Seán went down with a severe bout of malaria.

Next day we were up and about early. One of the most impressive early-morning sights in Tappita was to see a long crocodile of boys and girls smartly dressed in their green and white uniforms arriving at the school, having walked distances of up to seven miles. School began promptly at 8 am. Late arrivals were sent home, a discipline regarded as more severe than six of the best. Assembly began every morning with a salute to the flag and some well-chosen inspirational words from the Liberian Head of Discipline. I was asked to address the assembly on the first morning of my visit. Word soon got out that Seán's O'Pa would be speaking. Liberians love speeches and therefore hung on every world I said. My words were repeated many times throughout the day and recited to me time and time again at subsequent meetings, a courtesy which amused me enormously. I felt a little like Winston Churchill's second cousin, twice removed.

The students at St Francis, as at virtually every other school in Liberia, were expected to pay towards their education. In the absence of money, payment would often be in the form of a small pig or chicken. The pigs and the chickens would often be redistributed to those in greater need. The Salesians maintained the principle of self-help in all their work, disliking charitable handouts which only perpetuated poverty.

The clinic at Tappita was a hive of activity with a never-ending demand for maternity care, vaccinations, and treatments of every kind. Drugs were supplied by *Medicines Sans Frontières* (MSF) in Monrovia, ensuring that the people in the area had, at least, some access to 20th century medicine.

But nothing was easy. Back home, if you want water you just turn on a tap. In up-country Liberia, if you want good clean water you have to dig and mine your own well. While I was at Tappita I was co-opted on to the deep tube well project. Brother Donald had worked with a local 'diviner' to identify a natural water source. He had assembled an electrical motor capable of pumping the water to the surface. All he had to do now was construct a permanent shaft, lined with concrete cowling, to ensure a new supply of clean water. The cowlings were obtained with great difficulty and considerable cost from Monrovia. Two of these prized cowlings had already been lowered in to position at the base of the well. Eight more had to be lowered into place. This was a difficult task as each one had to be lowered manually, inch by inch, using a rope. Four of the strongest students acted as the winch-engine at the top of the well. Don stood at the base of the well and gave the command to lower each unit, guiding the descending concrete mass into place.

It was an amusing sight, watching this bearded Scot, barely visible in the bowels of the earth, hailing instructions: 'Lower away, lower away'. The third cowling was lowered gingerly into place. The fourth proved more difficult. It had reached halfway down and Don continued to call from below: 'Lower away, lower away'. The monstrous concrete mass gained speed and started to drop too fast. Don, frightened that the cowling might smash and worried that he might be crushed, shouted a counter command: 'Let go, will you let go!' By this he meant 'stop lowering the cowling', but he said exactly the wrong thing. The winch-engine four on the surface obeyed the command and let go. The cowling smashed down, destroying the three previously positioned units and pinning Don to the ground below. Snatches of Scottish abuse – 'You bloody idiots' – echoed up from the bottom of the well, while the four terrified lads fled as if for their lives.

Money was very tightly controlled on the school campus. Indeed, it was policy never to keep substantial sums there. However, from time to time it was necessary to hold a certain amount. While I was there US$2000 had been sent up from Monrovia to pay for a special project. Then the money went missing. The school's staff and pupils were investigated to no avail. The fathers put their loss down to experience. That evening, during the customary beer before the evening meal, someone suggested seeking the advice of the witch doctor. The old woman considered the question with due solemnity. She carried out a little ritual, conferred with odd-shaped fetishes on the sandy ground and spat copiously while she manoeuvred her hands over some animal bones. She cast some paraffin on a fire, causing flames to leap into the air, and solemnly pronounced that an inspection of the mango tree next to the main house should be undertaken.

No-one was prepared to be ridiculed by climbing the tree to carry out the inspection: that would be going along with the voodoo. Eventually, a small boy climbed up the tree to the top, where he discovered the $2000 in a hollow. The culprit turned out to be a newly appointed houseboy who had stolen the money, thinking he had secured an income for the rest of his life. Had I not seen this example of voodoo detective work with my own eyes I would never have believed it. It defied all reason. Then again, the sceptical side of my character was left with a lingering doubt as to whether the witch doctor had not been in on the job from the word go.

The thief was spared a severe punishment. He was lucky, because the local community could be unforgiving when it meted out instant justice.

Seán told me about a case of a youth who had stolen a chicken and was spotted by one of the elders who cried out: 'Rogue, rogue' – pidgin for thief. The chicken snatcher, only a boy, ran for his life, with the entire village in pursuit. He was finally cornered and given a severe beating. Had it not been for Seán's intervention he could have been stoned to death.

The children in Tappita were enthralled and fascinated by Seán's magic bag of tricks. Seán loved magic. He used to spend hours and hours practising card tricks and elaborate sleights of hand. Not all of them worked but he put so much energy into doing them, going 'Zap, Zap' like Tommy Cooper, that you always laughed.

Seán used magic as an effective way of gaining the children's confidence. His interest in children extended beyond the classroom. He was careful to ensure that every opportunity was taken to involve the less fortunate children of the town, including orphaned and street children. It was not uncommon for him to collect large groups of them outside school hours and conjure up a magic show combined with a geography lesson, followed by a bingo session which delighted the children's parents and the elders alike. It was a scene both absurd and delightful: Seán would call out 'eighty-eight' and the Liberians would sing 'Shut the gate.' Seán: 'Number Ten', the throng: 'Maggie's Den.'

My visit was soon at an end. In four days, we had packed a lot in. At the road blocks I had pretended to be a priest, then a very sick invalid; we had watched a witch perform detective voodoo and seen how not to sink a well.

I was due to leave Monrovia at 19 30 hrs on the evening flight to London. This meant leaving Tappita at seven that morning. As Seán and the team were committed to a heavy work schedule, I was to return alone. Fr John Thomas, who had an appointment at the leper colony, would accompany me as far as Ghanta from where I would undertake the rest of the journey by minibus.

John's own transport was a well worn pick-up truck. En route to Ghanta it developed an electrical fault and came to a dead stop, leaving us stranded for what seemed like hours on a remote dirt road. A large timber lorry came along and we managed to flag it down. The driver stripped down a wire cable holding the logs in place on his lorry and attached the leads to John's stricken engine. Two turns of the ignition and the engine burst into life.

At Ghanta I said farewell to John and boarded the eight-seater minibus with my 15 fellow travellers. The vehicle would have long gone to the knacker's yard in England and was far too small for its load. As well as the human cargo, it had to carry a number of live chickens, several large sacks of rice and wheat, baskets of fruit and vegetables, assortments of household items, a large table, a bicycle, a television and two small pigs.

I departed with my new-found companions, pigs and all, worried that we would not make Monrovia by nightfall. Five miles out of town the back axles snapped under the heavy payload. I traded up, arranging to do the rest of the journey in the luxury of a taxi, albeit one manufactured in 1956.

We travelled a whole ten miles before more trouble – a checkpoint. The soldiers wore dirty khaki fatigues and each one touted a rifle. The soldiers demanded a bribe from the driver. He told them he had no money. They appeared to let us go. As the taxi drove over the lowered rope, one of the guards pounced. He tugged at the rope causing it to catch on the rear axle. The rope pulled hard and ripped out the barrier posts. At this, two heavily armed guards swung their guns at us as the taxi came to a standstill. The driver and I were taken at gunpoint to the checkpoint commander and accused of causing extensive damage to the barrier. A large payment was demanded; otherwise the vehicle would be impounded. I argued our case, insisting that the guard had deliberately instigated the incident by raising the rope and that no payment would be made. As no payment was forthcoming I was told, with some menace, to repair the damage. The boss insisted that I dig fresh holes to accommodate the barrier posts and reconstruct the barrier. They gave me a penknife to do the job.

I inched my way on bended knees through stone and gravel, digging out the holes with the penknife. After digging and scraping for what seemed like hours, I had dug holes around 1½ foot deep. The posts were lowered and the holes carefully refilled and secured with the displaced earth. The boss then carried out his inspection of the new Dermot Devereux checkpoint barrier. He leant on the posts with all the energy he could summon until they were loose and unstable. They were not secure, he said, and demanded that the holes should be a foot deeper. I went at it with the penknife, pretty sure now that I would never catch that plane. Eventually, the holes were dug, the posts were virtually bomb-proof and the taxi was allowed on its way – with only 16 more checkpoints to go.

Somehow we made it. As the aircraft took off and headed for London my admiration for Seán and the priests grew. Liberia was not an easy place to do anything, even something as simple as going from A to B.

Seán, aged 7.

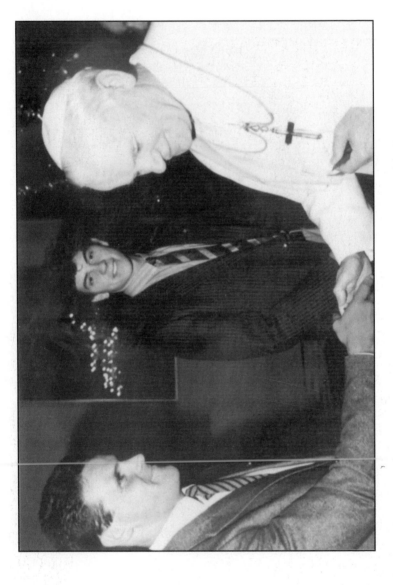

In January 1987, Seán visited the Salesian General House in Rome to attend a world meeting of Salesian Past Pupils. Here he met the Pope, the highlight of his visit.

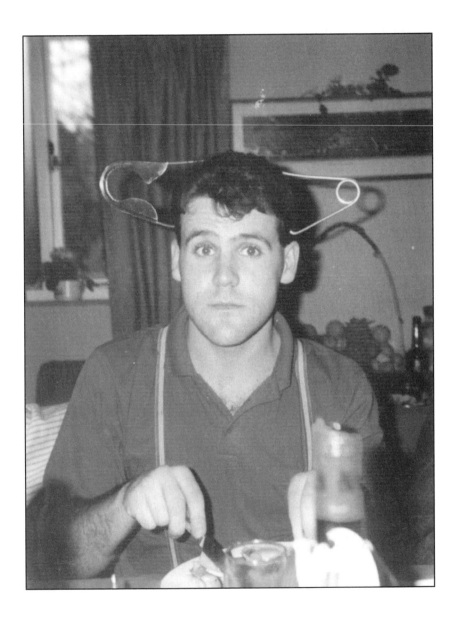

What safety pin?

Sign erected by Seán and knocked down during a later uprising.

The 'Killings Fields'
Liberia 1990.

Photographs by
Seán Devereux

Boy solider, Liberia 1990.
"Before you brought us the food, you sold us the guns,"
a chilling reminder by warlord to Seán.

Liberia.
The result of malnutrition.

Feeding station, Monrovia.

Last family picture.
Taken two nights before Seán died.
Nairobi 31 December 1992.

The Old Barn Resturant ~ Bagshot, August 1992.
Theresa, Tania and Seán.

'Year Of The Child' stamps.
Idea conceived by Melanie Agostini and Philip Cockrill.

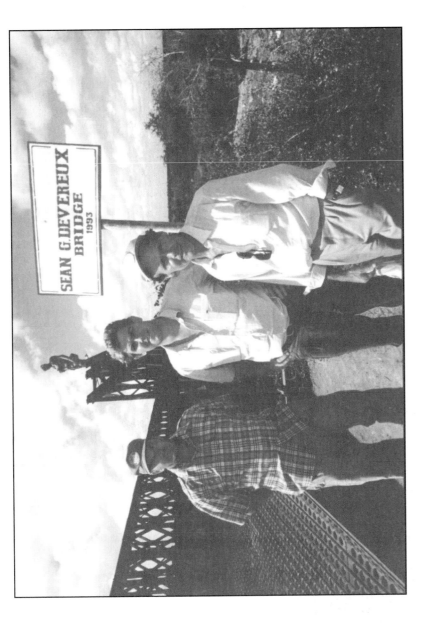

Mark Sterling & Dermot Devereux (centre & right).
At Seán's memorial bridge ~ Somalia.

LETTER FROM SOMALIA

Greetings to the Parishoners of St Swithun's, Yateley and to all my friends in the Salesian Provinces of England and Ireland.

A few words to keep you in touch on how your kind donations are being utilised here in the "Horn of Africa". I have heard some refer to Somalia as the Hell of Africa - I suppose a fair comment... but not entirely true. I took up a UNICEF posting here in September after concluding my time with the Salesians and the UN in Liberia. It seems that I have gone from the frying pan into the fire but I also like to think of it as an enriching, broadening experience.

No doubt you have been exposed to the horror pictures of starving children. Sadly it is a reality that has been brought about by Man's greed and not by natural disaster. There is no real drought in Somalia; it is a country which prior to the war exported rice and sugar in abundance; nomads wandered peacefully with their camels, goats and cattle living a relatively healthy life. Everything was then turned upside down because of the greed and ego of certain men. Siad Barre, the former dictator. Generals Aideed, Morgan and Ali Mahedi to so called warlords are the usual names mentioned in this battle of power. But one must add to the list: The US congress, the former Soviet Politbureau, the Italian and British Parliaments;- apparently a noble collection of men and women, who over the years approved the production and delivery of weapons of destruction to Somalia for its own self interest of course. So greed starts here.

Today in Somalia, in the southern port of Kismayo, I cannot walk from my house to my office (a distance of 400m) without heavily armed body guards. Thousands upon thousands of men in Somalia have their own weapons... they tell me it for survival. Boys of 17 years live out their Rambo fantasies, believing they are fighting for freedom. They are so blind... but who cares about children. In Kismayo, I wander through the market, checking on the prices of looted UN food; wheat, rice, beans etc and I see next to the bananas and camel meat, AK47's, kalashnicos, Barrettas, M16's, Bazookas, varying in price from $75 to $200 - all made in the so called 'civilised world'. Next door to my home is a shack with the sign SPARE PARTS, Sadly it is not for cars but for weapons, again made in the 'civilised world! We have a lot to answer for, and you at home can do something by lobbying your M.P's.

The relief work here is extreme in all senses. The needs are massive but the obstacles are also enormous. Normally the UN, ICRC and other n.g.o.'s have certain ground rules before they start to work. Such as reasonable security on the ground; Their own flagged vehicles that do not carry guns and the freedom to move and work independently to bring assistance to people that they decide are in need. Somalia is regrettably the exception.

Unicef, like every other relief group, are forced to hire gunmen to protect their offices and houses. We hire looted cars that are escorted by armed men in order to move around. We pay through the nose at every stage, to bring the donated relief items to the needy: at the port and airport for docking and landing fees, to porters to off load the goods, to truckers to transfer the goods to the warehouses and distribution centres. But sadly in many cases the beneficiaries are the market men and the various militias and not the innocent women, children and farmers who are the most in need.

The gun dictates everything here, and the biggest guns have the most power. Somalia now is simply lawless - The relief agencies -whose mandate is to reach the dying no matter what, acknowledge that we are subject to blackmail and extortion. But perhaps in some ways, by accepting this we are perpetuating the conflict by providing finance for these gunmen to go and buy more bullets which end up killing more people. The authorities which vary from place to place depending on which clan is in power, seek to involve themselves in our work, but only to squeeze us of every penny that we have. Essentially they are the black mafians.

Perhaps we have got everything wrong then. Maybe we should all pull out until the somalis with the guns allow us to work freely. And when the stubborn ones will not allow this perhaps the UN should send in what if they say no? perhaps the UN should send in _____

20,000 no-nonsense troops without ~~the approval of~~ the ignoring the warlords' objections and impose a safety chain ~~of~~ for the secure delivery of relief supplies. And perhaps we should ignore their ~~arguments~~ warlords' arguments that we are imposing on their own sovereignty, ~~and~~ because they know as well as us that the country ~~has~~ and its society has degenerated and fractionalised to such a bare level that arguments of sovereignty and self-dignity are now simply rubbish. (I know from talking to the average Somali citizen that they are crying out ~~for~~ for the UN to take over.

The reality is that the various relief groups stay and struggle with the harassment and intimidation because innocent children are dying of starvation now - and their presence does make a difference.

Unicef are involved in special Intensive feeding and health care for the severely malnourished and our supplies, brought in by German and Canadian air force Hercules are generally well secured. We tend to succeed in getting this relief through to the children and thankfully the feeding centres are now full of healthy and noisy ~~children~~ children. The general food distribution by ship however, is less successful. In our last consignment of 3000 tons of wheat to Kismayo less than 30% reached the target groups. We paid $160,000 US to trucking contractors, all armed militias of course, to transport the food with ~~food~~ elders from the various villages and towns who were supposed to escort the items. The food in most cases did not arrive, either because the elders made a deal with the truckers to divert the food to the market or because it was intercepted by a group of bandits with bigger guns. The one good thing is that the looted food does flood the market and the prices ~~drop~~ incredibly, now one bag of wheat (50kg) is worth 6,000 Somali shillings - about 1.00 US dollar - a price that many can afford, but still there are many with nothing.

In Kismayo today we have 50,000 displaced people, mainly farming families living in camps on the periphery of the town. They receive a cooked meal everyday from ICRC (a dry ration would only be looted). Now our aim is to resettle them back to their farms along a very fertile river valley only 150 km away - instead of reinforcing their dependence on us and allowing this pathetic waste of productive manpower. Unicef hopes to provide transport back to their homes with a resettlement package of food for 1 year, seeds for 1 year, material to rebuild their homes, tools to farm their land and raised community Health workers to ensure the appropriate distribution of Unicef drugs. By the next planting season, April 1993, we hope the displaced camps of Kismayo will have disappeared. But so much depends on security. These people will not move back to areas where there is fighting. The various clans must first agree to stop fighting. Time will tell.

Life for myself here is very up and down. I get so frustrated and fed up when I have to deal with the authorities & the guards or the contractors. Their greed is sickening. In contrast, I get such a lift when I get a chance to move out into the field and see how the feeding centres and health posts are running, and to regain contact with ~~the~~ more gentle face of humanity. Last week we cleared the excrement and nonsense of the town's football field and had a soccer and athletics tournament for the kids of the displaced camps. The Somalis can really run... one kid clocked 12·5 secs for 100m. Compared to the Liberians they were useless at soccer. Salesian school Chertsey u12 team would have beaten their Bo lads with ease. Next to the football pitch is an open field with hundreds of small dirt mounds. ~~They~~ These are the graves of children who died about 6 months ago. The contrast is so stark - but as I watched the energy and laughter of the children as they kicked the ball it brought home to me the message that where there is life there is always hope

TYPE ± COPIES TO.
- ① Editor - Simultaneous
✗ ② Fr Grogan - Provincial house in Stockport — suggest he may want to use snips of it for ?the Salesian bulletin - I fear this is too long!
- ③ Br Michael - Farnborough, (copies ? copy for old Salesians)
- ④ Fr Brian McGrain - Chertsey - for the school newsletter.
- ⑤ send me back 2 ? copies.

develop the ~~film~~ film - carry interesting snaps - copy to Fr Grogan.

I give him my address.

A voice that had to be silenced.

These two little chaps are friends of Seán's - one is four and one is six.
Whenever they heard Seán was in town they would trek
five miles to see him, crossing a dozen or so check points,
and then trek the five miles home at the end of the day.

CIVIL WAR

Word of the rebels' first move came to Tappita at Christmas, 1989. Rebel warlord Charles Taylor crossed over from the Ivory Coast into the eastern border of Nimba County on 24 December, 1989. The guerrilla forces expanded, split into factions and the conflict spread. In four years of war it is estimated that 100 000 people were killed and 2.5 million uprooted. The conflict continues.

The civil war did not start across the entire country overnight. It crept in, as the rebels took village after village and the authority of President Samuel Doe's murderous and corrupt regime seeped away.

What replaced Doe's government was worse: a crazy anarchy, with soldiers from one clan murdering the people of another. Liberia regressed very fast. Child soldiers, some wearing wedding dresses, spat out gunfire, thanks to the very latest western technology of death. And in the middle of all this was Mr Seán, trying to teach the kids geography, showing them magic tricks and hoping to organise an athletics competition.

The first serious indication that Liberia was heading for the abyss came in Monrovia in early January. Robert Phillips, an American who had worked for the Salesians, was murdered in the capital. The prime suspects were Doe's men, who probably killed Phillips in the false belief that he had been aiding the rebels. No inquiry was undertaken by Doe into his death.

Tappita was in Nimba County, the land of the Gio tribe and at the centre of the rebel heartlands. The Gios had been under the thumb during Doe's rule. Doe, an army master sergeant before he seized power in the bloody 1980 coup, was a member of the Krahn clan. Under Doe, many members of the Krahn clan were given the best jobs in the government and the army, while people from the Gio and other clans were frozen out.

On 12 November 1985, a former army general, Thomas Quiwonkpa, staged a coup against Doe and found support from the Gio people of Nimba County. He arrived from Sierra Leone with two dozen heavily armed soldiers, but the announcement on one radio station that Doe had been ousted was, to say the least, premature. The announcement led to jubilation in Monrovia, but Doe kept his cool; his troops won back the radio station, captured and killed Quiwonkpa. In front of a TV crew, Doe's soldiers bayoneted his corpse and ate his flesh in a barely credible cannibalistic ritual. Doe's soldiers, mostly Krahn, subjected non-Krahn civilians to beatings, extortion and murder. According to *The Rough Guide to West Africa*, for a week truckloads of mutilated corpses passed through Monrovia to be buried in mass graves on isolated beaches. In Nimba County, Doe's army staged bloody reprisals against the Gio. The ritual killing of the child that Theresa heard about on her trip to Tappita may have been one particularly ugly reprisal by Doe government forces against the Gio. For the Gios of Nimba County, there was blood to be repaid in kind.

No-one, that Christmas of 1989, knew just how bad things were going to get. On Boxing Day Seán left Tappita for England and a brief respite from the rigours of Liberia. He spent a couple of weeks at home at White Picketts, then joined Theresa, who was working as an osteopath at a ski resort in the Alps.

Theresa really noticed a change in him. He seemed much surer of himself and though he was still really lively and popular in the resort with all her friends, it was as if he'd found the balance between his spiritual side and everyday life. He was only 24. It was such a contrast from where he'd come from – lots of young people, drinking, going to discos, and Seán loved it. He taught one of the ski guys who worked at the hotel some Liberian pidgin – 'How dat body today, man?' – and they would shout it at each other when they passed on the ski lift. One day, Seán and Theresa hitchhiked to a nearby village, but no cars were passing. She moaned that they would never get a lift but Seán said, 'Yes we will, serendipity...' Theresa didn't know what he was talking about but at that moment a car drew up and offered them a lift. Things with Seán were like that. It was as if he was on the right wavelength.

Despite the fact that civil war was brewing in Liberia, Seán was determined to stage a major athletics competition for the country's Catholic schools in Liberia. His dream was to get a team to the Olympics. He had booked the Samuel Doe Stadium for the event in May. To this end, while in England he wheedled and talked his way into getting hold of lots of sports equipment generally unavailable in Monrovia, let alone Tappita. Lack of equipment was, of course, a huge problem for the Liberian athletes. By the time he was ready to return to Liberia, Seán had acquired a lot of kit. The problem was he had to get it from Gatwick to Tappita.

I helped to handle the first part of the journey: getting the stuff through Gatwick. It was not easy. One day he had appeared at home with a javelin, plus a starting gun and a shot putt. He was expecting to take the lot on the plane. His challenge to me – at that stage I was working as a manager for British Airways – was: 'Well, you know, Dad, you'll fix it because you know the run of these people at the airport and the javelin won't be a problem and the starting gun won't either.' The check-in staff member at Gatwick was somewhat perplexed when Seán and the rest of us turned up, complete with bulging suitcases, javelin, shot putts and what looked like a lethal handgun. We told her it was a starting pistol and only fired blanks. Seán wanted to take all this potentially lethal equipment as cabin baggage. Struck by his charm and enthusiasm, the woman used her discretion and minimised the excess baggage charges, but everything went in the hold.

I had fixed it in Gatwick; getting the javelin, shot putts and starting gun from Robertsfield to Tappita was up to Seán.

At the Ghanta checkpoint Doe's soldiers arrested Seán. The reason? He was bringing cannon balls and spears to Taylor's rebels... Seán demonstrated how to throw the javelin and how to putt the shot. The soldiers applauded, but then Seán was further delayed as they all wanted to have a go, trying to throw the javelin further than each other. The stand-off ended with handshakes. 'Yeaa, we enjoy you...' and a plea: 'Teach us good soon again...'

Taylor's rebels were inching their way across the map of Liberia, moving from the border region close to the Ivory Coast slowly, inexorably east towards Monrovia. Tappita stood directly in their path. The township was prickly with tension. The Gio people in the border region quickly abandoned the Doe government they hated and went over to the rebels. Doe's army could not defeat the rebels in battle and exacted retribution against the civilians of the wrong clan trapped behind their lines. The war quickly became both civil and tribal. The real victims were the ordinary Liberian country people who fled their homes for fear of being killed by the army or the rebels. Many walked to the safety, they hoped, of the more western areas of Nimba or over the border to the Ivory Coast or Guinea.

In a later interview with Margaret Percy of the BBC's World Service, Seán looked back on his time in Tappita during the late 1980s when the rebels were advancing.

'It was the talk all around. "The rebels are coming, the rebels are coming!" And there was a kind of excitement. You have to imagine, for three months we had lived under a curfew that had been imposed by the AFL, the Liberian army, and there was a strange tension already existing in the town and a growing resentment against the army's occupation because unfortunately they weren't a force for peacekeeping or for routing out the rebels, they were there – and I will say this plainly – they were there to make the people of Nimba County suffer. It was a good excuse [for the army] to steal their goats, their chickens; all their food just went, all their livestock went from Tappita and so there was this growing resentment building.'

Seán was in the thick of it, helping the people of Tappita endure the thuggery of Doe's AFL army. Father Larry described the slow descent into war in a letter to Seán, written after Doe's death. He told how a few days after Christmas 1989, Tappita started emptying out as families headed for their farms and the security of the bush. Harassment increased in town and eventually a curfew was imposed. People were locked in their houses in the heat from 4 pm till morning. There were beatings, arrests, looting, fear. Women and children fled town to stay on the campus. The AFL soldiers were scared among the Gio tribe. They interrogated and searched the priests' and workers' places, frightening them as rumours of atrocities flew.

According to Father Larry, Seán stood up to Doe's troops calmly. He lifted the spirits of the children by creating his own little world for them with magic tricks, singing contests, anything to distract their minds. He had a horrible monster mask he would put on, chasing after the kids as they screamed in delight.

Supplies got short; they shared everything. After a few short weeks several bullet-riddled cars came careering up to the clinic. A few Italians and some Liberians had been ambushed while coming from their timber company. Fr Larry recalls that Seán immediately asked pointed questions and got involved, as if he had been doing that kind of work all his life. Fr Larry kept in the background, watching with amazement. He and everyone else seemed so confused and not ready to act. It was almost the next day when some UN and UNICEF people showed up, and again Seán was very sharp at picking up what the situation was, wanting to help.

This was Seán's first substantial contact with the UN. He told the BBC afterwards that he had met up with a UN disaster relief man, Terry Lewis, who was planning to use St Francis as a safe ghetto. So Seán had gone down with him to organise a convoy to bring back. And, of course, while he was down in Monrovia, the school became cut off.

The day after Seán left for Monrovia with the UN team, the rebels under Charles Taylor abducted Fr John and a few days later, in mid-March 1990, they took Tappita. The chaos reached new heights. Seán was trapped in Monrovia, unable to help his old friends, while Fr John had disappeared into the bush. Eventually, he was freed and returned to Tappita, which the Salesians prepared to evacuate.

In a letter home written some time later, Seán praised the ingenuity of the Catholic Mission Network staff during the time of the chaotic rebel attack. They had, he said, provided a masterly support system by transmitting radio messages in Gaelic. Then the Liberians banned all radio traffic unless people spoke in English. Next, they came up with a code system which confused the rebels and enabled the operation to move forward.

Details of heavy fighting were relayed via a complicated code system, although the sisters sometimes confused the weaponry with the wrong code sign. The 'heavy crop of pineapples' (mortar shells) were confused with the 'lorryload of bananas' (machine guns). During times of rebel invasion and at the height of tension the nuns broke the code. Such was the case when the Leprosarium was under attack in Ghanta. The coded question 'How's the market in Ghana today, sister?' provoked the response: 'Well, there are a few pineapples around and lots of bananas in the market at the moment', followed by 'Oh Lord, there are exploding pineapples everywhere now and bananas flying through the windows!' Tragically, 70 of the lepers were later taken from the Leprosarium and shot because they were from the wrong clan.

With the rebels in charge of Tappita and law and order collapsing, the Salesians decided to evacuate the mission for a while. Fr John and the four nuns started out for Monrovia accompanied by a rebel escort. Their journey to the supposed safety of the Doe Government-held areas was tense. At one point the road was blocked by huge trees, felled by the rebels. They were cleared for a $25 fee. In the forest they picked up some refugees, dropping them off at Congotown, the first town held by Doe's troops. Sensing the tension in the town, one of the nuns feared that their Land-Cruiser might be strafed at any moment. She threw the refugees' bags out of the vehicle, and with them Fr John's bag containing the Salesians' funds, US$4000 in all. The money was never found, but the party was lucky to escape with their lives.

Around midday the Tappita mission group was driving along the dirt track when suddenly they met Seán coming towards them in a three-ton open truck, flying the UN flag. Seán had been recruited as a local worker by the UN's Terry Lewis and had borrowed the truck so that he could attempt to rescue the priests and nuns. The two parties screeched to a halt, jumped out of their vehicles and, ignoring the danger from ambush, stood there hugging one another and laughing with relief. They were safe-ish.

Seán's first UN boss, Terry Lewis, was no wilting violet, but a former officer in the SAS who had served in the Falkland Islands. He had extensive logistical know-how but the problems of feeding so many refugees forced from their homes was immense. As the front-line slowly moved east across the map of Liberia, crops were abandoned by terrified farmers and finding enough food to eat became a huge problem for the refugees. Seán, with Fr Larry helping out, often went up country from Monrovia, distributing as much food as possible, but to do the job properly he had to go very close to the front-line, then just short of Gbarnga, 120 miles from the capital. There was often no way of knowing where the front-line was.

The danger of ambush was real. Fr John, who had made his way safely to Monrovia, remembers warning Seán about the dangers: 'Seán, the rebels who are coming down that road aren't going to advertise exactly where they are and sooner or later you could just drop right into it, so be very, very careful!' Seán had replied: 'Of course we're careful'. Fr John was worried because he suspected that Seán didn't believe they would shoot at a UN-marked vehicle and, moreover, that the UN chiefs in Monrovia did not know just how risky the Liberian hinterland had become.

It was around this time in early April 1990 that Seán met Michael Emery, who was to become a lifelong friend. Michael was a hefty Australian of Irish and Lebanese descent. After four years teaching in a Christian Brothers school in Australia, he realised he was beginning to feel a little fraudulent just standing in front of a classroom teaching social justice in an armchair fashion, so he decided to do something. In 1989 he wrote to the Christian Brothers saying that he would like to do volunteer work and they suggested Liberia. Michael didn't know anything about the country, but had said yes anyway. All he could find out was that the main exports were rubber and iron. However, the day he left Australia on a plane bound for England, en route to Africa, he read a small paragraph in the newspaper headlined: '5000 killed in Liberian civil war'. He thought that if it was anything serious the Christian Brothers would contact him.

When he arrived in Monrovia in February 1990 Michael asked the two Christian Brothers who picked him up at the airport about the civil war. They said that it was nothing serious and it was just the Doe Government troops exerting themselves in Nimba County. He started work as a teacher at the Gbarnga Christian Brothers School, roughly midway between Monrovia and Tappita.

He and Seán met on 19 March, 1990. Michael was the coach for the athletics team and Seán came out to do some guest coaching. The way he took the kids and taught them long jump and so on amazed Michael, whose first impression of Seán was that 'he had a great sense of humour and was just bursting with energy and a terrific natural way with children. Afterwards we had a couple of beers and our friendship just seemed to click.'

From then on, the pair were inseparable. Both got jobs with the UN, immersing themselves in the mass refugee crisis as Liberia's society and economy collapsed under the strain of the civil war. Michael was the diplomat, Seán the energiser. They had a loose relationship whereby Michael would do all the politicking and negotiations with relevant ministers. He'd organise the guarantees and the OKs, the go-aheads and the documents, then Seán would get out and do it.

Michael was always there to support Seán, who carried into the hinterland not a Kalashnikov but a bag of magic tricks. The UN food truck not only brought food but an opportunity to restore broken spirits. Michael's powerful frame often succumbed to the power of Seán the magician. They had a trick in which Michael would disappear through a trap door in the flatbed of the truck and reappear behind the crowd as the magic cracker exploded in Seán's hand to the yell of 'Abracadabra'.

Liberia also worked its own black magic on Michael's stomach. Once he consumed a snake and lizard pie Seán had procured. This had roughly the same effect as Seán's magic cracker as it caused Michael to make lightning exits from the truck to the bush toilet. Thereafter, the UN food truck was known as Emery's Relief Truck.

The war came steadily closer to Monrovia as Doe's troops failed to quell the rebellion. In late April 1990, Seán wrote to his old friend, Sarah Healey. The letter gives a flavour of his despair at the turn of events, but also shows that he still made an effort to create fun and good humour amid the misery.

'Greetings from sunny – no – enchanting – no – I'm afraid to say war-torn Liberia. This place has really become a mess. I'm sorry for being so poor at corresponding over the last few months but matters here have been very preoccupying!'

He told Sarah how the rebel incursion in January had now blown up into a major war; four weeks earlier the aid workers had had to evacuate their mission in Tappita as the rebels took over that part of the country. Prior to that, there had been plenty of 'excitement'. The two priests Seán was living with had been held by the rebels for three days, the sisters had got caught in an ambush. He found the whole thing so sad: 200 000 people had fled the county (Nimba), the Salesian school and clinic were now left deserted. The Liberian army was, in Seán's words, 'vile'. Under the curfew it had harassed, killed and stolen from the Gio people who lived in Nimba County. The Salesian teachers were put in jail, all the goats in Tappita were stolen by the army. It really was an eye-opener for Seán. As a result, many of the people joined up with the rebels and they succeeded in taking over practically half of the country.

Families were split up, people were homeless and hungry. Seán's own students and families from Tappita walked for two to three days through the bush, away from the fighting. Seán had joined up with the United Nations, which kept him from 'going cuckoo and doing nothing in Monrovia'. He was involved in food distribution for all the Nimba people who had been displaced and were staying in other towns. On the day he wrote the letter, he was off to the border with Guinea where many refugees had settled.

All the other lay-volunteers – Irish, English, Australian – who were working in the Catholic schools were now 'displaced persons' staying in Monrovia. Seán found the company fantastic, and they had spent a day at Hotel Afrique, sipping gin and tonics in the pool. It was a real escape. 'Don't spread that one around too much,' Seán wrote. 'I want to preserve my image of roughing it up in the jungle for the good of the needy.'

But he did spend a great deal of time roughing it in the jungle and in the capital. Seán and the others worked 24-hour days to organise a massive food distribution for 60 000 displaced people. The athletics competition was cancelled as the Samuel Doe Stadium had been converted into a distribution centre. Figuring out how to feed 60 000 was a logistical nightmare. Carefully selected and trained supervisors were positioned to ensure that the stadium was divided to accommodate the different tribal groups. Elders had been assembled to ensure that their people received the correct allocations of rice and oil.

Seán had devised an ingenious classification and coding system to prevent people taking two lots of rations. But some of the refugees were equally ingenious at devising ways of circumventing it. Police and soldiers alike were commandeered to control the crowd. Long convoys of food supply trucks were positioned on the road leading to the stadium. Care was taken to ensure that every truck reached its destination, in case it took a wrong turning en route. But hungry mouths were to be denied. The day before the feeding programme was due to get into full swing, disaster struck. Seán later described the desperate situation in May 1990 to the BBC:

'At that stage the Gio people were being victimised, they were being sought out and killed. They were blamed for backing the rebels and so the Krahn soldiers, the AFL, had started to attack Gios around the city in Monrovia, which was now full of refugees. They didn't feel safe and a number of them decided to take refuge in the UN compound – up to a thousand people.'

On the night of 28 May, the AFL came in, captured 30 people and killed them. Their bodies were found the next day. It was a brutal massacre.

Seán and his team were there, ready to start a huge feeding programme in Monrovia the next day for about 60 000 displaced people, and they had to cancel it because the UN insisted it could not stay there. The aid workers' security wasn't guaranteed – some of the UN security guards had also been shot in that raid.

Seán told the BBC how Doe had come the next day and actually stood on the steps of the UN and talked to the people. He said, 'You are my people. I'm here to protect you.' He even offered them sanctuary in his own mansion. Seán was incredulous. Some of the women then started hollering 'You're killing us', and at that point Doe was whisked away by his security men. So then the people left and went to the various churches scattered around: the Lutheran church, the Methodist church, the Catholic Salesian Centre.

But the sanctuary of the churches was not to be respected.

The evening after the UN compound massacre, Seán and his colleagues were ordered by the UN to evacuate. They assembled in the German Embassy and were airlifted out to Dhaka in Senegal from a small airstrip in the city of Monrovia.

One of Seán's distribution supervisors was there at the airstrip to say goodbye. 'Now we will surely die, Mr Seán,' he said. 'All our careful laid plans are for nothing; the soldiers will take everything, our people will perish.'

His words reinforced the pain and anguish Seán was to endure. Unfolding below the steep climb of the aircraft was the scramble for the spoils of war. Rice sacks, oil, canned food and medical supplies were ripped from the convoy of trucks by Doe's soldiers.

Seán felt he had let the starving down.

'HE BIN PENDING'

Seán and Michael spent most of June and July 1990 in England, recharging their batteries at White Picketts. Maureen recalls how Seán soon got into the swing of family life and had parties going every day. He was a great family binder. All the aunties, uncles, everyone came round for barbecues. Sometimes it felt like a bit too much for her to cope with, but he loved the light side of life.

At home, Seán talked a lot about the daft, funny and moving things that had touched him in the civil war, but was much quieter and more withdrawn about the dark side of life in Liberia. Perhaps this was because he sought to protect his mother, sisters and me from the stress and fear he must have suffered himself. You had to drag it out of him to find out what he really went through and even then, we never knew exactly how awful it was until too late.

As Maureen sensed, Seán was always drawn to challenge. He couldn't abide sitting around, just doing a nine-to-five job. The extreme challenge of the aid worker's life had seized Seán's imagination and sense of justice.

Seán and Michael returned to Africa in late July, to work in the francophone state of Guinea, which curves round Sierra Leone and sits on top of Liberia in the map of West Africa. Many Liberians had fled to Guinea for sanctuary but there they found little charity.

Shorty after Seán and Michael arrived in Guinea, news of a shocking massacre in Monrovia broke which showed that the situation in Liberia was going from bad to evil. In late July Taylor announced that President Samuel Doe had been deposed. The declaration was false, but it caused Doe's jittery troops to go on a blood-letting rampage. On 29 July, a gang of Doe's soldiers, high on alcohol, attacked around 600 mainly Gio refugees crammed into the Lutheran Church. Fr Brian Jerstic and Fr Larry Gilmore, both of whom had remained in Liberia, heard shooting and screaming in the night but could not move for fear of being shot. The next morning they found 320 corpses, many of them women and children hacked to death or shot, and a few surviving babies underneath the bodies of their mothers who had lain on top of them to protect them.

The Lutheran Church massacre impelled yet more Liberians to flee the country, but life was no better in the neighbouring countries.

Seán later described the ups and downs of doing aid work in a corrupt and heartless Third World country. He and his fellow aid workers had been evacuated to Gambia and Dhaka in Senegal, where they waited to be recruited back as UN volunteers. The security situation was not good enough for them to re-enter Liberia, according to the UN, so they were deployed in Guinea to help with the refugees next door, assisting in the World Food Programme (WFP) to try and ensure everything was going right for the Liberian refugees. 'I don't want to be sensational,' Seán wrote, 'but while I was there between August, September, October, all I can say is that the situation was shocking in terms of the level of corruption, absolutely deplorable. There are no other words for it.'

The Guinea government had masterminded the system. They had control over the number of refugees admitted. They controlled who was going to be distributing how much and where. And they had manipulated the agencies, so local Guinean people were being fed at the expense of Liberian refugees.

Seán was based in the Guinea Forestière region, where most of the refugees had gone. He described a situation in which 140 000 people were declared as refugees in a town of 80 000 inhabitants like N'zerekore, even though there were probably no more than 40 000 refugees. So the food for this 'surplus' 100 000 people was going to feed the local Guineans or directly into government hands, or to profiteers. Seán said that the Liberians didn't have the chance to get the food because they didn't have the ability to pay for registration cards that were being held by the Guinea Red Cross. He saw many of his students up in N'zerekore, Mandingo students (from the Mandingo tribe) who'd had to flee Tappita. They were coming to Seán, a UN official, saying they couldn't get their food because they weren't prepared to pay their 15 000 Guinean francs to the heads of prefecture or the government people to get a card. The most frustrating thing for Seán was that if you objected, if you spoke out, you got expelled from the country. It was as simple as that.

They went to one place called Youmou where they were told that there were 11 000 refugees; this was the figure the government minister had come out with. And it was an emergency. The road was so bad there that the food hadn't reached the people, so Seán and the other volunteers decided to do a rapid registration and a rapid distribution of food. They went along with the Guinea Red Cross, which was the implementing agency, and took over the registration process – very strict registration to identify whether the refugees were Liberian or not. They came out with a figure of

3000 to 3500 – way below the official figure that the government had stated. And because they stuck to the figure one of the people with them, Mr Alberto, who was working with the League of Red Cross, was expelled from the country while the other UN volunteers were restricted to their house in N'zerekore and were refused movement because they had 'insulted' the Guinea Government by disagreeing with their figures.

Seán's anger at the corruption in Guinea was not synthetic. He wrote to Michael Winstanley, the Salesian Provincial in Stockport, England, describing the situation.

Some of the stories from the refugees were horrific. Many trudged through the bush for days, even burying their dead and giving birth to their babies there, in the hope of reaching the borders. Large numbers fled from Monrovia to Macenta via Sierra Leone. Rebels massacred many people in a Mandingo Chiefdom in Lofa County. Voingama, a rebel leader, authorised the slaughter of about 65 Mandingos who had stayed in the town thinking the rebels were friendly. The rebels looted on a sweeping scale across the country. 'It is really tragic,' wrote Seán.

He explained how, in the first few months of the conflict, the NPLF (the rebels) had been respectful, small and tightly controlled. Now it had grown out of control: children had weapons and tribal revenge was rife. However, they were failing to quell the flow of refugees into the border areas. The refugees were very damning of the Mandingos, who had collaborated with the army in January/February by going around identifying the Gio/Mano troublemakers.

In Seán's house in N'zerekore, there were six St Francis lads from the mission in Tappita working for them – cooking, cleaning etc. As Seán said, they were 'Mandingo but very Liberian'. They hated Guinea, and really wanted to go back to Tappita; all their best friends were Gio or Mano. But if they travelled back now they would most probably be killed.

At the time Seán was writing, most of the Gio/Mano refugees had returned but just recently there had been a flood of Krahn people out of Grand Gedeh. The NPLF had secured the county the previous week. 'It has been good for me to see the other side of the conflict,' Seán wrote, 'to be associated with people who really supported Doe. It gives me quite an insight into tribalism.'

Michael Emery remembers how bad the corruption was, how the Guineans just saw an opportunity to make sackloads of money. Some people were making tens of thousands of dollars. For example, when the Red Cross rep first arrived in N'zerekore and he got out of the bus, he had a small bag, a really old T-shirt and an old pair of pants. Within two months he had three or four taxis operating in town, designer suits and sunglasses, and a big house with a generator. That was the kind of money that was being made out of the refugees. Seán and Michael's job was to monitor what was happening. They were feared because they would roll up in town, go through the books and talk to people. It got to a stage where they'd promptly be arrested in every town they went to. They'd say they wanted to see the warehouse and the men in charge would say no.

One day they decided to get away from N'zerekore, go to a supermarket, have a cup of coffee and come back. Spotting a whole load of UN rice going into someone's house, they asked the man if he was a refugee and he said no. Seán said, 'What's this rice doing here?' So they got arrested.

Seán later told the BBC that he couldn't cope with Guinea Forestière and had asked to leave before he was expelled. He painted a vivid picture of how bad things could be.

At Conakry, the coastal capital, a ship called the *Santa Rita* had arrived with the first refugees from Monrovia at the end of October. They had suffered terrible injustices and seen dreadful things going on in Monrovia.

A great flood of people were coming out by ship after ECOMOG – the West African peace-keeping force sent in to impose a ceasefire, comprised mainly of Nigerian troops with contingents from Gambia, Ghana, Guinea and Sierra Leone – had come in to secure the port. Seán was in Conakry when the first ship came in with 3000 refugees, many of whom were of Guinean origin. After their gruelling five or six-day journey, they were left on the quayside for four days, restricted by containers, where they were refused food and water. According to the Guinean authorities, they had to be security checked as they came in. So these refugees were in Conakry, surrounded by UN people and relief agencies who weren't even allowed to get in to make sure they were well looked after.

One of the Guinean soldiers stood on top of a container and got fresh water from a pipe on the other side of the container. He lifted it over into the area where there were thousands of people who had just come off the ship, and exchanged the fresh water for the remaining goods that these people possessed – a radio or $50. 'It was just unbelievable what they were doing,' said Seán. 'The culture over there has been so hardened to make a buck whenever they can.'

The aid workers managed to get in and give the refugees assistance, pulling out the dying ones to send them straight to hospital. When the next ship came in, they were already there on the pier with their packages of food relief and water all ready; before the soldiers could put their restricted area around they had got it all set up. And that was it, the soldiers couldn't do anything about it. While the aid workers were there it was very difficult for them to exploit these desperate people; it was a question of presence.

It is difficult to describe the justification for or the purpose of foreign aid workers risking everything in desperate places. Seán's work supplying water and food to the boat people of Guinea-Conakry is a hard-to-beat explanation of why people like him are needed. Their presence made things better. The numbers of dead on arrival (DOAs) reduced while those in bad medical condition and those born at sea (BAS) were plucked from the hatches as soon as they arrived. Mothers received postnatal care and were reunited with their newborn.

Human rights violations in Guinea were commonplace. The authorities were suspicious of the Liberian refugees and this easily slipped into brutal paranoia. In Conakry Seán discovered a group of 25 young men who had been tortured and held as political prisoners. He took photographs of their sickening injuries. Many of the men had cigarette burn scars on their backs. As a UN worker, he was able to provide medical care, food, clothing and rebuild the confidence of the prisoners, but he could not raise this matter directly with the authorities and retain his job. So he sent the film and the details of their tortures to me and I forwarded the case to Amnesty International. Thanks to pressure from Amnesty on the UN (with a little help from Seán), the Liberians were released from prison.

His worst memories were during those early days when each ship arrived. 'It was like looking into hell.' When the aid workers opened the hatches they were forced back by the stench. A multitude of faces and hands reached skywards. They had to lower a large box-cage over the hatchway with a crane and distribute the food from an aerial position. On the dockside, they had a number of refugees working with them on a food-for-work programme. One of the workers attempted to conceal rice in his clothing, but was spotted by one of the guards who gave chase along the dockside. A greasy rope foiled his escape and he went over the side. No one was able to save him because of the heavy weight of rice in his jacket and he went to the bottom, to his watery grave.

One aspect of the aid workers' job was to be food monitors. They had to go out and see what was happening and who was getting the food. They sent back report after report after to the World Food Programme showing that there was a great deal of corruption going on there. The UN was in a very difficult position because the Guinea Government would make anyone who made waves persona non grata. That happened to Mr Lamberto, an Italian colleague of Seán's working with the League of the Red Cross. He was given 18 hours to leave the country. So that was the conundrum. Did you speak out and get thrown out of the country? Or did you accept a certain level of corruption in order to get some food through to some people?

There was a further complexity. The amount of cheap rice washing around Guinea, thanks to falsified and corrupt accounting, meant comparative riches for the aid-gangsters running the profiteering racket. But the practical effect was to knock out the bottom of the rice market, crippling the local subsistence farmers, some of whom helped with long-term western aid programmes. Seán knew this and could see the obscenity of it: another reason to speak out against injustice.

Seán's forced exit from Guinea could be read as evidence that he lacked the diplomacy necessary to be a good aid worker, but the extent of the corruption in Guinea was so gross that, sooner or later, any honest man would have had to say: enough is enough. Nor, to be fair, was Seán the first aid worker to be slung out of Guinea.

He moved to Sierra Leone, to the west of Liberia, to help with the Liberian refugee crisis there for a short while, but by mid-November he had gone back to Liberia through the only route in – by US Marine helicopter. Doe had been murdered in September and his death videoed, but his faltering and cruel regime had been replaced by a messy and violent anarchy. By late autumn, no-one was in charge of Liberia. The country was open to gun law, its fabric ripped apart by war.

Seán wrote to us a few weeks after his return:

'Today the buildings in the Sinkor district (of Monrovia) are splattered with bullet holes. For months the rebel faction fought along this front line in an attempt to move the government. They themselves lost the discipline and focus and massacred many innocent civilians on the other side of the tribal divide. Today the coconut trees in the city lie sprawled across the ground. The people in their starvation sought to extract the palm cabbage that lies within the trunk of the tree. It is a powerful symbol of the desperation faced by the hungry civilians.'

He told Margaret Percy of the BBC the story of his return to Monrovia. The first three aid workers had gone back by American helicopter on 16 November. It was still very tense in the city. A ceasefire just held, but they needed an ECOMOG convoy/security escort down into Sinkor, which was just half a mile away. In the city there were people looking severely malnourished with swollen feet.

Michael Emery could not forget the horror of Monrovia on his return: 'When we came into Monrovia the city had been besieged for about five months and there was literally no food there. People had eaten all the palm trees, dogs, cats, birds and lizards that there were.' It was estimated that about 60 000 children had already died of starvation when the aid workers went in. It was a really desperate situation. The UN did a nutritional survey and there was 37 per cent severe malnutrition amongst children under five.

In November/December Seán told the BBC that, although he didn't see fresh bodies on the street, going through parts of the city he was constantly aware of a stench, 'a kind of cheesy something' that came from fresh corpses.

At the beginning of December Prince Johnson got a bit nervous and decided to go and finish off the rest of the AFL, so there were two days of chaos in the city again. He broke the ceasefire and fresh bodies littered the centre of town. Seán reckoned the majority of the victims were civilians, and he knew that half the army of the AFL had been wiped out – over 2000. In the beginning stories were rife about checkpoints held by the AFL: 'Gio – put him aside, shoot him.' Then, at the NPFL checkpoint: 'Krahn – put him aside, shoot him.' This was very common; the skeletons were there to prove it, even those of babies and tiny children.

Seán himself almost became one of the skeletons at that time. It happened on his birthday, 25 November 1990. The next day he met Michael Emery at the American Embassy, saying he'd had enough. He'd just spent the night in jail at Prince Johnson's camp.

It is hard to give the full measure of the mind of rebel warlord Prince Yormie Johnson. In Liberia he was well-known as the psychopath of psychopaths; there is a video to prove it.

The best-selling video in Liberia in the early 1990s was 'The Death of Doe', an indescribably gruesome film, shot in real time on 11 September, 1990, depicting the torture and murder of the country's president as Prince Johnson looked on. One sequence from the video was described by *The Guardian* correspondent, Mark Huband, the following month.

' "Cut off his ears," Prince tells his men, his hands held in semi-prayer. He doesn't say it loud. The camera swings to the victim. The rebels stand on his body, lying him flat. A knife flashes in the bright lights. The camera gets close. The knife saws through the screaming president's ear and the ritual has begun.'

Visitors to his camp reported that Johnson, out of his mind with drink, would cry out to his servants 'Bring it out!' and show off the president's head to general wonderment. The video gives some idea of the cruelty and madness into which Liberia had plunged.

Johnson had no particular regard for foreign workers. In August, 1990 he didn't like the look of a French aid worker, Jacques Montouroy, head of the Catholic Relief Service in Monrovia, who was working with the ICRC (the International Red Cross), and a local Liberian, also with the Red Cross.

Johnson accused them of selling rice on the black market. He had them chained together. Then he personally shot the local Red Cross worker, once to wound, twice to kill, ignoring the distress of the Frenchman still handcuffed to the corpse. Eventually the Frenchman was released and evacuated from the country. Seán doubtlessly knew about the killing of the Red Cross man and the presidential snuff movie. They were the talk of Liberia that autumn.

That November Seán went to Prince Johnson's camp to discuss the reconnection of a water supply to the city of Monrovia. At the end of the meeting, as Seán was leaving the compound, he was intercepted by one of his old students from Tappita school. The boy had been kidnapped and forced to become a boy soldier. He dropped his gun, ran to Seán and said: 'Please, please, Mr Seán you have to get me out. This is an evil place.' The boy, like many of his classmates, had joined up and come under the power of rebel leader Prince Johnson. Child soldiers were common to all the rebel factions. Charles Taylor had even established what he called the 'Small Boy Unit' (SBU).

Seán presented himself to Johnson and requested the release of his young pupil. Johnson was positioned in a rocking chair, feet atop a large wooden desk. A half-empty bottle of spirits stood alongside a Kalashnikov on the right side of the desk. Behind was a drape tapestry of the Holy Family and sacred music blared from a ghetto blaster in the corner of the room.

'Why you come back?' asked Johnson, his brain befuddled with alcohol but vaguely remembering Seán from their earlier meeting.

'I want to take this boy back with me. He is only nine years old; he is frightened, terrified of fighting in battle. He wants to go back to school in Tappita, he wants to find his family, his brothers and sisters. He's just a small boy,' pleaded Seán.

'How do you know Tappita? Where you come from?' enquired Johnson.

'I am a teacher, I have been working at St Francis' School in Tappita. This boy is one of my students,' said Seán.

'Oh, you a Tappita man. You from Nimba County. Oh, you our friend. I am Nimba County man too, my village near Tappita. OK, OK, you take the boy now, but you bring him back some time soon, vaaary soon. This is his home now,' insisted Johnson.

'No, if I take him now, he will leave the gun behind. He will stay with his family, he will go back to school, he has to forget all he has seen here,' insisted Seán.

Reluctantly Johnson agreed, called the guard and signed a piece of paper endorsing it: 'OK to take this boy, signed Brigadier General, Field Marshal, Prince Johnson'.

Seán and his driver collected the terrified boy and left the compound in the UN jeep. They had only travelled a distance of five miles when Seán sighted in his rear mirror an open land rover, travelling at speed behind them and containing armed men. They were dressed in wedding dresses and wearing long blond wigs. After firing warning shots over the UN vehicles, they overtook Seán on the inside and forced his vehicle off the road. Johnson's bodyguards, most of them drunk, announced that Seán and the boy had to go back. Seán, his driver and the boy were taken at gunpoint back to the compound.

Seán was dragged before Johnson, who had now deteriorated into a drunken stupor. 'Why you take this boy?' Johnson demanded.

'Because you agreed it was OK for him to come with me,' replied Seán.

'No, you can't take him. We know your tricks, you are a CIA man,' retorted Johnson.

'This is ridiculous. You know we were with you today, the other UN official and myself, discussing the water project,' Seán reminded him.

'Bring the boy,' Johnson commanded the guards. The weeping boy was dragged in and placed before the psychopath. As he cowered on the floor, Johnson removed a revolver from his belt, placed it under the boy's chin and commanded him to stop crying.

Seán intervened: 'He's only a boy, he's frightened.'

'No, he is a soldier boy. Soldier boys don't cry, do they, boy? If you cry I pull the trigger and then you cry no more,' said Johnson. The guards laughed approvingly as Johnson drank the dregs from his bottle and breathed into Seán's face.

'You are a CIA man. You want this boy to spy on us, but we are vaary vaary clever for you. Now we beat this boy and put you *kwi* in the jail house.'

Johnson reached for the empty bottle, missed and collapsed in a drunken heap on the sofa. Both Seán and his driver were taken to the jail and dumped into a cell. They sat there as midnight passed and Seán's 26th birthday dawned.

But Michael Emery recalls how Seán related even this bleak story with his usual verve and humour. When Seán got to the jail, the jailer asked him, 'Whitemon, what are you here for, whitemon?'

And Seán said, 'I don't know really.'

The jailer became slightly hysterical, crying: 'I've got to put a reason, otherwise they'll shoot me.'

So Seán said, 'Just put "pending" down there and he spelt it out for the man. All through the night Johnson's guards kept coming along and saying, 'What the whitemon in jail for? Uh hug? He bin pending. The white men they can pend before the war and they can pend after the war, they can pend too much.'

They were released the next morning.

Michael, laughing at the memory, says, 'Seán always told that one with a bit of a smile.'

Caroline Tanner recalls Seán telling her, after his night in jail, how he had got a kind of perverse kick out of standing up to Prince Johnson, the ultimate bully-boy. She also remembers his remark that he was plagued by feelings of guilt because, as the UN white man, he would always be safe, protected, unlike the young boy he had tried to rescue.

At the time, neither of them was aware of the terrible irony of his words.

SOMEBODY'S CHILD

It had been nine weeks since we'd last heard from Seán. His 26th birthday had come and gone on 25 November. No letters. No telephone calls. No messages relayed by returning aid workers. Communication with Liberia had always been difficult, but now with the civil war raging it was virtually impossible. We began to get worried.

Eventually, the long silence was broken by news received via a ham radio enthusiast that Seán had been involved in an incident with the rebel leader, Prince Johnson, who had now taken over part of Monrovia. The radio ham said that Seán had gone to Freetown in Sierra Leone to set up a communications system with the UN and to establish a 'rest base' for the aid workers. I sent a message via the ham saying that I was coming out and would see Seán in Freetown.

I snatched some time off work and set out for Freetown, but without knowing for sure that Seán was there. On the plane I met up with two businessmen who were fortunately heading in the same direction and offered me a lift. It was pitch-black when the plane touched down. In spite of the darkness, broken by car headlights, I could see that Freetown was a shocking hole, worse even than Monrovia, with the roads honeycombed with craters and the houses dilapidated. Not surprisingly, Sierra Leone is reckoned to be the second poorest country on earth.

I had been told that Seán was staying in a UN rest base in St Michael's, which was on the coast some distance from the capital. It turned out to be a much longer and more arduous journey that I had expected. After we crossed a huge expanse of water on a jam-packed ferry, my new friends dropped me at a garage by an intersection and sped off into the night. As the red brakelights of their Land Rover disappeared into the night, I felt a little forlorn standing on my own on a pitch-black road in Africa. There can't be a bloody hotel out here, I thought to myself.

By the garage there was an ancient Morris Oxford with its mudguard askew; inside a sleepy driver dozed against the wheel. It was after midnight when we set out and the second part of the journey, negotiating the portholes, took an hour. Had I known the way, I could have walked it in half the time.

We reached the hotel just after 1.30 am, and I went straight to reception to check that Seán was actually there. He wasn't. The reception had no record of any Seán Devereux. There was a group of cottages occupied by a UN team, including Terry Lewis, but my son was not on the hotel register. I felt a sinking feeling in my stomach because I feared my journey had been in vain. In my despair, I worried that my message via the radio ham had not got through. My mind was working overtime, wondering what I was going to do next. I decided to check into one of the hotel cottages and try and find out where on earth Seán was the following morning.

Deflated, I ordered a few beers. The hotel, patronised by French holidaymakers, was surprisingly upmarket compared with the shambles of Freetown. Whitewashed cottages perched on green lawns a few yards from the ocean. It wasn't the kind of place I expected to find Seán. I sat on the hotel wall overlooking the beach as the waves lapped the sandy shore. The night air was full of the hiss of the surf, the chorus of the crickets and the croak of bullfrogs.

My thoughts were interrupted by a Swedish voice: 'It's a very peaceful place, but it's a bit hard to sleep at night. Have you just arrived?'

I turned to see a youngish man lighting up a cigarette. 'Yes,' I replied, 'the journey took me a lot longer than I expected. The roads are a bloody disgrace.'

'That's true. Are you here on holiday or business?'

'No. I was hoping to meet up with my son. He's working with the UN but he's not here,' I said, my voice full of disappointment.

'You're not Seán's father, are you?' he said, excitedly.

I wasn't sure I had heard him correctly. 'Seán, do you know Seán? I can't believe it!'

'Yes, of course, we've been waiting for you all day. Seán's right here. He's sleeping in Terry Lewis' cottage. Terry went back to Monrovia this morning.'

'Well, I'm damned!' I said, taking his hand and shaking it vigorously as if he was a long-lost brother. We went straight to Terry's cottage. I poked a stick through the open window and lifted the mosquito net at the end of Seán's bed.

'What a way to welcome your father!' I called out.

'What? Bloody hell! It's old Gerry boy!' he said, using my old RAF nickname. He jumped out of bed and was through the door, slapping me on the back.

'You made it, you old devil...'

'Enough of that, where's the beers? Did you get my message?'

'Yeah,' he said, 'it was the last thing on the agenda at yesterday's UN crisis meeting. "Seán's father arriving Freetown". '

We talked through the night and watched the sun rise over the ocean with the help of a crate of beer. We had breakfast at dawn and slept until midday. That afternoon we went for our customary run. Our route was about five miles along the road, then back along the beach. The locals were bemused to see me running with Seán and they called out: 'Oh, the old man, he running with the son.'

Along the road, we were joined by a number of Sierra Leone businessmen, dressed up for work in pin-striped suits, bowler hats and briefcases. They jogged along with us for a while, one announcing: 'I am very happy to run with you' and another: 'Running will make my journey faster.'

Towards the end of the run, Seán upped the pace, putting his old dad under pressure yet again. Half a mile from the hotel we were hailed by a gang of young African boys offering freshly cooked fish outside a hut. Seán, intrigued, came to an abrupt halt.

'Got to see this, it'll only take a minute.' The boys surrounded us and showed off a rich variety of fresh fish, all of them presented in Tupperware containers and displayed on a plastic tablecloth. There were no customers.

'OK,' said Seán, 'you've got it all wrong. Now, we're going to change everything. Forget the Tupperware, get rid of the plastic tablecloth. We're going to cover your hut with green banana leaves. You must dig a hole in the sand for the fire and serve the fish in the banana leaves. Use your local wooden bowls for the salad. All we need now is some African beat with a little French music and you'll fill the place every night. Don't forget to cut the coconut shells in half and put candles inside for a little atmosphere. We'll put up a notice near the hotel, saying 'Opening tonight'.

Thereafter, the hotel restaurant suffered a loss in custom as the French holidaymakers made their way along the beach to 'Le Bon Companion'.

Seán had lost a lot of weight and, though in good spirits, he had clearly been through the mill. There was an ulterior motive to my visit, of course. I put it to him that he had done his bit, and that for the sake of us, his family at home, he should start thinking about another job or settling down with a wife, or doing anything which didn't involve spending a night in Prince Johnson's jail. He listened and told me he wanted to carry on for a couple more years and then he would stop. I left him surrounded by a swarm of African kids.

Life in Liberia was not all hell, not at all. Seán and Michael Emery worked very hard at making fun amid, and sometimes of, the chaos and misery. Other aid workers did not escape their wicked humour. They nicknamed one 'the Grim Reaper'; others were the constant butt of silly practical jokes, such as having spiders put in their beds. At weekends, when the work stopped, it was party time.

Caroline Tanner first met Michael and Seán in December 1990. She recalls that it was Michael's birthday on 17 December: 'I didn't know anyone very well but I could see that Seán was totally dynamic. He was never in one place for a minute. I remember thinking: God, he's intrepid. He knew the Liberian lingo and he was a really good dancer.' Caroline was particularly surprised to find that Michael and Seán had all the party trimmings, including cocktail shakers, which Seán juggled behind his back as if he was a bartender in some Manhattan dive-bar. 'I had never expected Liberia to be so much fun,' she says.

All the foreign aid workers used the same radio frequencies for security and each had their own radio callsign. Michael was 'Southern Cross', Seán was 'Shamrock' and Caroline was 'Pink Gin'.

Michael and Seán were 'like Tweedledum and Tweedledee', according to Ofeibea Quist-Arcton, the BBC's West African correspondent, who first visited Liberia's civil war at this time. She had met Shamrock – Seán – and Southern Cross – Michael – on her first trip to Monrovia in December 1990. They'd said: 'Look, you know, you're not here for very long. Can we just drive you around to show what's happening here and the sort of things we're trying to do?' So they drove her around and she got a vivid picture of Monrovia: painfully thin children, suffering from malnutrition. The city was devastated, the people starving.

Seán was a bit of everything, says Ofeibea. At the port, where he organised the off-loading of the food, he was very efficient and hard-working, but he worked equally hard at having fun. In the middle of the crisis in Monrovia he and Michael organised a Christmas party because their feeling was: yes, we're in a disaster area, yes, things are terrible, but we've got to try and live as normally as possible. 'There was a real effort not to get too bogged down, not to get too depressed by what they were doing,' Ofeibea says. 'They made a big effort to work hard and after a day's work they were very good at entertaining.

Ofeibea noticed that Seán was like a magnet to the children, especially in Monrovia, which was where she saw him operating. He'd drive up in his UN pick-up and they would swarm around him. 'He was like a Queen Bee with the drones all moving around him and he loved them,' she says. She remembers Seán's room was full of footballs and magic tricks that he got sent from England. He'd put a whoopee cushion on a chair and get a child to sit down; there would be an almighty farting sound and the children would burst into peals of laughter. That was the way he saw the children of Liberia, the way that would rebuild the country.

She says, 'I can still hear the children calling out their popular Liberianised version of Seán Devereux's name – "Shuh, Shuh, Mr Shugh" – as they swarmed around his UN pick-up truck.'

On Christmas Eve Seán and Michael went out dressed in Father Christmas outfits, handing out sweets and UNICEF jigsaws to the street kids. Afterwards, there was a party for all the aid workers. Ofeibea was there, and she saw Seán dancing for the first time at Christmas. He was decked out in an African boobo dress like a sort of chief, with a hat and everything, and he was just sweating because he was taking everyone on, all the women, all the men, all the children at the party. 'He danced us off the floor,' she says. 'It had to be seen to be believed. He was incredible, so energetic. You haven't seen anything like it.'

Very occasionally, the stress of the mass killing and a country disintegrating in front of his eyes got to Seán. Caroline Tanner remembers the work Seán put in from late 1990 to early 1991 to organise the efficient off-loading of food at the port. He was off-loading food and had got a good work-for-food scheme going. The more the people off-loaded, the more they got. At the beginning it was very disorganised, a real free-for-all scramble with people stuffing rice into their pockets, but Seán really got things moving. He was in control without being hated.

But one particular man always gave Seán a lot of grief and finally Seán exploded, hitting the man. He came back in a real state, saying to Caroline: 'I can't believe I did that. I can't believe I did it. I just hit someone. I've never done that in my life. What have I done? I've lost control... '

Seán and Michael had both gone out to Liberia to teach in Catholic mission schools; in the new year of 1991 both ended up digging mass graves. One of their jobs was to bury the dead that littered Liberia. The fresh corpses were the worst. If you could see flesh, clothes, says Michael, then you could imagine some personality.

Seán photographed what he and Michael saw: heaps of skulls, hundreds of them, lying higgledy-piggledy. Some were intact, some perforated by single bullet holes, some stacked in tidy rows on the ground, some in a wheelbarrow. The photographs painted a picture, irredeemably bleak, of a shattered society.

Seán later told the BBC that close to the airport they found hundreds of bodies, hundreds of skeletons picked dry. They buried about 200 there, who had been killed by the AFL (loyal to Doe) because that was their killing field. Then, as the area opened up through ECOMOG control, they managed to expand out and came to places such as Dupont Road, which was held by the NPFL. And again the same story: hundreds of skeletons at the end of this killing field. Most of the bodies in the airfield would have been Gio/Mano, and most of the bodies in Dupont Road would have been Mandingo/Krahn.

There was also the zoo. After the people had finished eating the animals in the zoo, that area was used as a killing field.

In such circumstances, even the most compassionate people have to distance themselves if they are to keep their sanity. 'It's funny, said Seán. 'I mean after a while you become kind of immune to it and it doesn't strike you. I do remember the first time I went there, feeling sick. But then after that it was just a question of...you drop them in. We had our UN lads here and they swept them up and buried them. The Father came down and gave some kind of religious something at the burial. We would have covered at least 500 bodies in those three centres.'

Seán erected a sign above the mass grave and asked Fr Joe Brown of the Salesians in Monrovia to give a blessing to the bodies. The sign read: 'This is a mass grave for the innocent victims of the civil war in Liberia who were killed because of the tribe they belonged to. May they be remembered so that it may never happen again.'

Seán gave an interview to a UN camera crew as he walked through the killing fields, pointing out human bones, bullet holes, bullets. These words are taken from a page of the UN transcript with the original spacing retained. It could almost be a prayer or a poem:

'There it is.
Somebody, somebody's mother or father or
brother or sister.
Could be a child.
There's one here.
Vertebrae, no, they're quite big.
That was a small one.
There are the bullets.'

Maybe something else kept Seán sane in the killing fields. Michael recalls they laughed a lot. 'You had to maintain your sense of humour. Seán loved life. He loved children.' In Liberia a four-year-old and a six-year-old walked for miles, crossing six checkpoints, just to hang out with Seán; then they would trek back home again at the end of the day. He had boundless energy and ideas. 'You can imagine the effect of his magic bag of tricks,' says Michael. 'We'd bury the dead during the day and at the end of the day he'd go out and perform tricks for the kids.'

But Ofeibea sensed that Seán *was* deeply affected by the work of having to bury so many dead. She spoke about this in a conversation with Richard Alwyn, the producer of the BBC Everyman documentary, 'Mr Seán':

'It was devastating. I mean, to go to a country to help, you go to be a teacher, and suddenly you're engulfed in a civil war. It was hands on things like digging trenches to bury hundreds of skeletons and skulls...after a while he felt pretty numbed by it all.' She remembers him saying, 'You know, sometimes I don't feel anything. I'm burying human beings, children, women, men and I don't feel affected by it.'

Ofeibea reckons that if Seán had allowed himself to become totally depressed by what he was doing, he would have ceased to do a good job. 'I guess after a time you just have to decide, well, this is a job. But then maybe when you go home and you've buried all the bodies, all the remains, then you allow yourself to relax, and then you must know... You remember how awful it is. It must be hard to deal with.'

Alwyn went on to talk about the effect of the suffering on Seán. He'd seen a lot of video clips of Seán, who was a big joker in the early days, forever giving two fingers to the camera with a great smile on his face, but more serious towards the end of his life. Did he grow up through it? wondered Alwyn. Was the suffering a part of him becoming a more mature person?

Ofeibea replied: 'Seán was always a big joker. That was the good thing about him. He was able to be deeply serious and he was able to be deeply silly. He was such fun but it's true that you can't live through Liberia and it not have an effect on you.'

What she found astonishing about Seán was that, though he'd seen all this death and destruction, people he knew killed, people he'd known before the war – probably very gentle, honest, upright people – turning into rebels, his faith never wavered.

'I don't know whether "deeply religious" is how I'd describe Seán... He was somebody who believed in something. It's true that he was a Catholic, a practising Catholic, but he had a much deeper faith. He believed in something and he thought that ultimately it would come right. It might take a long time, it might take years even, but ultimately all this was for a purpose. I'm not sure that I went along with him but we agreed to disagree.'

Theresa also reflected on how Seán coped with working in the killing fields of Liberia: 'I can't think about Seán without also thinking of his closeness to God. His faith was strong. It didn't weaken, even in the face of what he witnessed in Africa. In fact, it gave him strength. He never blamed God. He blamed the weakness in human beings. Catholicism clothed his spirituality, but it was not the tight, drab, uncomfortable clothes of repression, guilt and piety which people sometimes think you have to wear.'

In February 1991 the Gulf War started against Saddam Hussein and Seán finally succeeded in staging the UN sponsored Fund Day, the athletics event at the Samuel Doe Stadium which he had planned the previous year. Caroline Tanner recollects how Seán instigated and organised the whole event, a sports day for 1000 orphaned and war-traumatised children.

He spent all the time shouting instructions through a microphone. He had roped in everyone, all the aid workers, to do various jobs, and had even got the ECOMOG band; everyone marched in behind them, Olympic style. The Irish Goal girls gave out the Coolaid – soft drinks – and other aid workers were on the time-clocks. Caroline got locked in the ice cream van which was being bombarded by kids. She couldn't get out as the door was jammed, and someone had to rescue her.

At the beginning of the main race there was a false start. Everyone ran off, bombarded the T-shirt hut and stole the 'I've completed the race' T-shirts before the race had even begun. Seán went mad and yelled at everyone to get back to the start line. 'It was screamingly funny,' says Caroline.

But as Michael Emery saw, there was a serious purpose behind the fun. Seán gave the children more than food: he made them feel they had something to live for.

Seán wrote to us from Monrovia on 8 March 1991, giving a graphic account of his work there. He was totally absorbed in the operation. The work was very time-consuming and demanding – he felt he had never worked so hard before – but he loved it. The only problem was that he had no times of quiet and silence – 'contemplation (spiritual or otherwise) has no look-in,' he wrote. 'Such a contrast to Tappita.'

A typical day for Seán started at 8 am, briefing his 25-strong Liberian UN monitoring team, who checked the 168 neighbourhoods to ensure the information submitted on the food-claim directory was correct. 'You wouldn't believe the corners of corruption, right down to the grass roots. I could write a book on my detective discoveries; some are hysterical.' In their last distribution he'd managed to get rice, oil and beans out to 700 000 people, that is, everyone had got food; 163 distribution centres were now working and their only problem was authenticating the registration. 'Right now I whizz around the city with my criminal investigation squad, UN monitors, mainly ex-Tappita teachers. Some of the neighbourhoods are masters at creating ghost houses and inflating occupancies.'

They had over 30 supplementary feeding centres in the city, and another ten orphanages – UNICEF had started a field hospital which saw 200 patients every day. So all and all, the relief programme was working. Seán's real concern now was that Liberians might develop a dependency on aid. 'We therefore have to stop the general distribution and leave a food-for-work program intact.'

Seán makes the feeding of 700 000 sound like a commonplace. In the middle of a savage and chaotic civil war in West Africa, it was not. At the time of his death in Somalia, there was some muted criticism of Seán that he was undiplomatic and lacked political awareness of the consequences of speaking out. But there can be no question as to his ability as an organiser.

According to Michael Emery, Seán was regarded by the UN and by other aid agencies as 'probably the *crème de la crème*'. He was held in very high regard because of his organisational ability and his cultural sensitivities, the way he worked. He worked exceptionally well with Liberians, and preferred working with them in the field than working in the office with the UN fat cats.

Perhaps his greatest gift was his dynamism. He single-handedly organised the feeding of the 700 000 people in Monrovia; by getting two teams to compete with each other he managed to raise the amount of food that was moved from 150 to 180 tons a day. 'If he had lived to 60 he could have changed the world,' says Michael.

In his letters to England, Seán spent an enormous amount of space on letting everyone know how much fun he was having. A letter dated 8 March 1991 was no exception:

'Life here has really lifted up with refreshing new arrivals of relief workers. Concern and (Irish) Goal are now operating, and sure aren't they a great crack!

'Last night we had a great party at 'Goal', the Irish NGO, amid a tropical storm. We drank our way through a few cases of Club beer: the brewery, believe it or not, is back in operation, nearly at full capacity.'

That Sunday he had escaped from the management of food, people and logistics to take a UN truck out to the beach with street kids from the Save the Children shelter or the orphanage run by UNICEF/MSF. He had managed to squeeze '142 kiddiewinks' into the truck. As usual they got up to a bit of mischief and managed to smuggle the odd door frame from the deserted houses on the beach, which they used for firewood back at their night shelter in the city. These street children, aged between 7 and 17, survived by 'hustling'. They had been largely displaced by the war and had what Seán called 'an incredible street-wise mentality'. What they really needed, he felt, was a constructive programme of Day Care, and he was hoping to get the Salesians involved.

As the frontlines of the civil war stabilised a little and the ECOMOG troops expanded their presence, it became possible in the spring of 1991 for the UN workers to leave the (comparative) safety of Monrovia for the hinterland.

The trips upcountry were never easy, as Michael Emery recalls. Most of the rebel soldiers, especially the young ones, were very influenced by what he regarded as 'junk media – Rambo and Terminator and things like that' – so they had this image that anything western was good. Often the aid workers would get to a checkpoint to find somebody wearing a gas mask or a wedding dress with a wig and earrings, and these were guys with guns. So it was, as Michael put it, 'always an interesting experience' going through a checkpoint.

One thing that really disturbed Seán was the fact that the former deputy head of the school where he had been teaching in Tappita became a checkpoint commander. He was quite shocked that somebody from a Catholic school would actually join the rebels and stay with them. But he and Michael always had a good laugh as well. Often, they'd be very sarcastic towards the checkpoint soldiers, who were completely unaware of it. Seán would say things like: 'Oh, I enjoy your nail polish today. That's beautiful. That's fa-i-ne.'

The motivation for the children becoming soldiers was simple, according to Michael. Often they would join because a member of their family had been executed by a different rebel group. There was one 17-year-old boy, Philip Clinton, whose father had been a Customs Officer executed by Taylor's troops because he had worked for the Doe Government. So the son joined Prince Johnson and he had to undergo certain initiations, one of which was 'bullet-proofing'. Once Philip was accepted into Prince Johnson's army, he was expected to follow orders, which often entailed executing people from the opposite tribe. He actually executed a Mandingo woman, the Mandingos being loyal to the old Doe Government. But when he was ordered to skin somebody alive, he wanted to leave Prince Johnson's army. Something inside him told him that was inherently wrong. So he left Prince Johnson's army and asked Michael and Seán for a job.

The minds of the child soldiers had been poisoned, said Michael. A lot of the children would go into battle drugged, he remembers, or they would be at the checkpoints drugged or drunk on local cane juice. One chap stood out. He was 13 and called Easy Killer. Seán – this was the kind of person he was – told him that if he disarmed and came down to Monrovia, he, Seán, would pay for his schooling. Seán was constantly encouraging these children to be normal, as normal as possible.

Seán was on the first ECOMOG/UN 'confidence-building' probe out of Monrovia to NPFL (Taylor's) heartland in Gbarnga, roughly midway between Tappita and the capital. First of all, the party met Taylor and his wife in a 'real propaganda tour'.

Later, Seán caught up with his old pupils. When he reached Gbarnga he heard a couple of people shouting out of the window 'Mr Seán, Mr Seán'; it was his own students from Tappita who had made their way to Gbarnga as part of the NPFL, the rebel group. He guessed that about 80 per cent of the boy students over Grade 5 from his school had joined up. To Seán it was frightening and so sad because he'd seen them playing football and being 'untouched' up in Tappita. And here they were, because they were mainly Gio, because they had suffered under Doe in 1985 when the attempted coup failed. They called it a 'disadvantage': 'We had to join because of the disadvantage'.

There had been a huge amount of pressure put on people up in Nimba, who were Gio and had then come under rebel control, to join up. Seán saw so many of his students armed with Kalashnikovs and Berettas, but when they saw him they ran and gave him a big hug and said they wanted to go back to school. They wanted the thing to be over. But, of course, when their chief commander said 'step in line' they'd play along and continue.

Yet Seán realised that a lot of the kids enjoyed having control and power. Up in Tappita they'd had nothing to do all day long but go to video centres with portable generators and play games such as Exterminator, Predator and Rambo. Now, in the middle of the rain forest, they actually had the opportunity to live out the fantasies they'd seen on TV and video, and played on-screen. A lot of them really did love this chance to be Rambo. For Seán, this factor was central to a lot of the children's participation in the killing.

'I now have a feeling of anger,' Seán told the BBC in an interview, 'real anger at people like your man up there, Charles Taylor, and all the other rebel groups that they can take on children. OK, they feel they have a just war, fine. *But why use 13-year-olds?*

Seán's whole trip to Gbarnga was devastated when he found out that two of the kids in his class were dead, killed in battle. The two that had died had been the most gentle boys, not macho aggressive types. One of them had gone jogging with Seán every day, and he was a good left wing. 'It's such a waste,' said Seán. 'This boy was used in this conflict and he was killed by an ECOMOG man. It's just so stupid. And so, having felt so sad, I feel kind of angry now.'

Michael remembers Seán's sense of loss at the death of the two lads: 'I remember he was as upset as I have ever seen him. He just rammed the window up in the car and cried, and that really threw him for a few days as well. I guess it was the evil of recruiting boys into the army, and that affected him in a really deep way.'

In a letter home, dated 18 March, Seán went into greater detail about the two dead schoolboys. One, Arthur Monweh, aged 16, had lived behind the mission in Reeves Hill. He was an altar server and 'one of the gentlest boys you could know'. Now his body was rotting in some area where

ECOMOG had fought. The other boy, Lester Troho, was a tailor's son in Tappita. He had made Seán's beige trousers, but now he was dead and would never come back. 'I don't think I have ever felt such sadness in my life, I'm frustrated at the patheticness of it all,' wrote Seán.

He wondered about the role of the mission now, and any other development organisation, especially after witnessing the efforts and work of a lifetime wiped out within one year. Was there any point to it all? 'Last week I had the attitude, well, sod them all, let the country rot,' he wrote, 'but now I feel different.'

Through his personal experience of Gbarnga, now more than ever Seán felt the need for real mission work, effective education – an attempt to broaden people, especially the young, so that they could develop with vision and a respect for life. 'You can't just leave or desert these children. They will be left totally confused and potentially maladjusted. And real attention needs to be given to them and a school set-up is the best place to start.'

Seán's mother sensed the depth of his despair at the killing of the two child soldiers. He saw lovely, soft-hearted children who had no choice. They had to go and fight for freedom – for so-called freedom – and this really broke his heart.

But, as ever, in the midst of despair and depression, Seán and the other aid workers fastened on to the absurdity and comedy of war to pull them through. Caroline Tanner remembers one such weird event, the kind of thing they used to talk over and laugh at in their spare time, or at weekends when they all met up in Monrovia.

She was travelling with Denise Barrett, another aid worker, and some others in a different car from Seán, and they got separated. Caroline's group ended up getting stopped by Taylor's men at a checkpoint and held for several hours. Their suitcases were searched, at which point Denise got really angry and threw her underwear at the soldiers. The checkpoint guy began saying, 'That girl is hitting me with her underwear, arrest her.' Caroline says, 'The whole situation was so stupid it was funny.'

Sometimes there were eight-year-old kids manning the checkpoints and they could be the most dangerous. Often they would read your papers upside down. Caroline would carry round a huge tub of paracetamol and a bag of sweets and dish them out, which helped calm things down. 'It was stories like the knickers one that would keep us all going amidst all the horror,' she said.

It is strange but true that many of the recollections of Seán's fellow aid workers dwell on the light side, his humour and infectious love of parties and fun. One story, which could well be a tall one, is that, held up at gunpoint at a roadblock, Michael and Seán broke the ice by handing out condoms and telling the soldiers they were 'a new type of chewing gum'.

The dark side may have been pushed aside in memories, but the horrors were real enough. As 1991 progressed, the UN and the other aid agencies slowly penetrated the rest of Liberia. In the hinterland, they found that the Krahn people – loyal to the late President Doe – were now very much under the thumb of the rebels. Many had died; the survivors were starving. One of the surreal difficulties aid workers like Seán had to confront was that very few in the outside world were interested in an African civil war as the West went to war against Saddam Hussein. Yet the horrors of Liberia were every bit as real as those of Iraq.

The level of harassment against Seán and the other aid workers ebbed and flowed with the political tide. In June 1991 Seán gave an interview to the BBC World Service in which he complained about the brutal oppression of Taylor's soldiers against the Krahn people, former supporters of President Doe. This interview enraged Taylor's 'Minister of Health', Dr Gbokolo, who was, in fact 'responsible' for health only in the messy inkblot of Liberia under Taylor's control. Dr Gbokolo wanted to ban Seán from working up-country – doing his job of monitoring that the UN's food supplies got to the starving – because of this interview. After a lot of diplomacy, Dr Gbokolo decided not to ban Seán.

That summer, Seán and his driver, Bobo, were arrested by Taylor's soldiers and accused of taking photographs of a military truck. They were held for 20 hours, but even this became something of a joke.

At the end of August the chaotic situation worsened when Taylor's territory was itself attacked by a new militia, made up of Doe's old AFL, the United Liberation Movement for Democracy in Liberia: ULIMO. Around this time Ross O'Sullivan and David Copley of GOAL went missing in the Cape Mount Bomi region, only to reappear, having been released by Taylor's rebels. It was a working environment in which a slight slip of the tongue or an angry gesture at a roadblock could get you arrested or banned or worse.

Seán wrote home on 29 September 1991, describing some of the terrible things he had seen and some of the jobs he had to grapple with. It amazed him that after nearly one year in 'this relief business' there were people still starving. The problem with Grand Gedeh, he felt, was that it had only just opened up to outsiders. The remnants of Doe's army who fled Monrovia put up pockets of resistance to the rebels, who really did avenge the wickedness of Doe by making the whole of his Krahn tribe suffer in Grand Gedeh. Seán was practically the first relief worker through the zone and the UN had started a relief programme there.

The majority of the population was still hiding up in the forest away from their villages, which had been burnt by the freedom fighters. Now Charles Taylor (whom Seán had met for a half-hour chat in Gbarnga) was embarrassed about Liberia dying of starvation in areas under his control, so he had told all his commandos down there to behave and let the people come out of the bush. This was not easy when there was a deep background of tribal mistrust. Now, with the aid workers' presence, the NPFL behaved better and the Krahns felt a little more confident. Seán's work had become more rewarding.

The political changes at that time fascinated Seán. Two weeks before he wrote to us, all the relief groups had been accused of spying for the CIA by Taylor's men. There was an incursion from Sierra Leone by another group of rebels, and any relief workers in that country were 'obviously' undercover agents or collaborators with the invading force. The rebels were 'uncouth and uneducated', they knew nothing about the Geneva Convention and basically did whatever they wanted. Seán had been detained for an hour by Special Intelligence forces of the APFL in Gbarnga and had some ludicrous accusations made against him. Luckily, he had been given access to 'President Taylor' in a planned meeting, so he brought this issue up and Taylor promptly sacked the head of National Security.

But any other Joe Bloggs had to suffer the consequences and the key commanders at the gates were now even ignoring Taylor's orders. Things were falling apart for him. Taylor had recently been forced to agree to ECOMOG being a peace-keeping force throughout the whole of the county and for his men to be disarmed and encamped, thus paving the way for free and fair elections. It is easy to imagine the indignation of these local warlords at being told they had to 'surrender'. Seán felt that there might be an internal coup against Taylor now, and that if ECOMOG acted swiftly, the future could be really bright.

ECOMOG did not act swiftly and the military stalemate carried on, listlessly. Liberia had disintegrated into Monrovia, controlled by ECOMOG, and the hinterland, sometimes called Greater Liberia, which had fractured into a number of small, hopeless statelets, each run by a tribal warlord. None of the warlords had the military muscle to dominate the others, so the country was left twisting and turning in a dance of chaotic limbo.

EXILE

During the autumn of 1991 Caroline, Michael and Seán travelled to the south-east part of Liberia. Caroline remembers the horror of discovering so many malnourished children, but also the light-heartedness created by Seán's love of practical jokes and magic:

'Seán was wearing an old man's mask and a Liberian came in to where they were staying; he took one look at Seán and ran out screaming,' she recalls. 'Seán chased after him, then ripped off his mask, to the Liberian's astonishment.'

He had hundreds of tricks with little balls and coins that used to appear in his hands. His tricks would frequently go wrong, but he loved doing them anyway. And he didn't just do the tricks. He would dress up in black tie and tails and put on a show. For Seán, the bigger the crowd the better. It was a kind of showing off, but it must have been a release for him. And it brought the Liberians and the other aid workers wonderful moments of fun and innocence in the middle of the war.

And then – disaster.

Seán, Michael and Irish aid worker Ross O'Sullivan were all in Zwedru, south-east Liberia, doing work that was largely unsupported. There was no-one to say 'slow down, back off'. They were working in very highly stressed areas and had to be 100 per cent fit and able, and of clear mind all day, every day. They could never have a bad moment because what they said and did would be taken literally. Before Ross had started working for the UN, he had gone to them and said: 'You can't let people go up-country on their own. They have to be in pairs, even if one guy just sits on his arse and does nothing all day.' That guy would be there for that five per cent of time when his partner was not totally with it. The aid workers in Liberia were only ever as safe as their ability to defuse a situation, as they would invariably be faced with some form of conflict at any time.

Seán had been working very successfully in Zwedru, which was further down the main road from Monrovia than Tappita. Before the war, Zwedru had done well because it was the home area of President Samuel Doe. It even had, according to the indispensable *Rough Guide to West Africa*, a place to stay, the You and I Motel, two cook shops (the Cool Cabin and Kings and Queens) and three discos – Roots, Travellers and, best named of all, the Checkpoint. The war did not serve Zwedru's nightlife. Hitherto, the area had prospered because of the Doe connection. Once President Doe was murdered, the NPFL troops loyal to Charles Taylor butchered many of the local Krahn people, who fled to the bush for safety. In the autumn of 1991, they were beginning to come back to villages and towns near Zwedru, but Taylor's troops controlled the city itself with an iron fist. The atmosphere in Zwedru prickled with tension.

What happened next is best set out in Seán's formal report to his UN boss:

'Letter to UN Co-ordinator, Emergency Relief Operations in Liberia, Official Report. Incident Report – Zwedru. 13 December 1991.

'(1) UN Team arrives in Zwedru 7.00 Tuesday evening 10 Dec. to embark on the third general food and farming tools distribution for Grand Gedeh – carrying 96 tons of food. Convoy is stopped at the checkpoint in the middle of the city, outside the Catholic Mission – UN warehouse. [Taylor's] Commandos insist on searching all vehicles. I am surprised and shocked at their aggressive attitude. I explain the policy of no-search of UN vehicles and furnish them with a written statement of the agreement reached in Kakata on 25 October which clarifies that UN vehicles are not to be searched. The agreement is disregarded. After some considerable delay, in which our ten-ton truck is searched, the UN team reaches the UN house in Zwedru.

'(2) The distribution schedule is set. All villages and towns "out of town" to be supplied from Wednesday 11 December though to Sunday 15 December and Zwedru City be supplied on Monday 16 December. Note: all towns and villages are populated by Krahns [pro-Doe, anti-Taylor] returning from the bush after over a year's hiding in the high forest. Zwedru is now predominantly Greho and at least 30 percent of the city's population belongs to NPFL [pro-Taylor, anti-Doe] families.'

The situation was therefore fraught with difficulty because the Taylor troops in Zwedru town knew that food going to the towns and villages outside was destined for their blood enemies, the Krahn people. The troops in Zwedru had a strong incentive to impede and stop UN aid reaching the Krahn people, even though the aid shipments had been agreed with Taylor and the Krahn, including children, were starving. This would have been obvious to any of the UN management team reading Seán's report. Moreover, it was clear that Seán knew what he and his team were doing.

93

The aid convoys were planned so that they went out to the outlying Krahn people first; only when these sensitive deliveries were completed would the pro-Taylor people in Zwedru City get their supplies on Monday 16 December. Seán's report continued:

'(3) Friday 13 December – all the UN vehicles are involved in serving villages and towns south of the Putu Mountain. IE Jawadee, Geeblo, etc. UN-14 and UN-19 need to reload back in Zwedru for a 2nd trip to Jawdee in the afternoon.

'Friday 13 December, 2.45 pm: UN-14 is stopped at the central checkpoint. The food items have just been loaded from the warehouse, 30 metres away. All 20 bags of rice and 25 cartons of fish were ordered to be taken off the vehicle and put on the sidewalk. Commandos confiscated one bag of rice and one carton of fish, stating that it was for them.

'3.20 pm. I arrive in UN-19 and observe the scene, patiently waiting and saying nothing. The rice and fish are returned to the car including the confiscated items. The pick-up is still refused permission to pass so I go over to the commander to inquire.

'They are now not happy with the personnel travelling in the pick-ups: UN driver Anthony Teah and Friday Tashor, a rice loader from the Sanpo tribe. Commandos refer to the tribal identity of the rice loader and demand to see his documents which entitle him to load rice for the UN!

'They refuse to allow the car to pass until I produce a list and identification cards of all my local casual labourers, ie rice loaders, gardeners, cooks, carpenters at the UN house etc. After lengthy discussions I agree to submit a list of all local personnel involved in the relief effort but that the pick-up should leave first. The pick-up departs.

'3.50 pm. UN-19 now loads its consignment from the warehouse. This is watched by commandos Elijah Dopo and Suehn Weah sitting under a tree 30 metres away. Loading is completed.

'4.20 pm. UN-19 leaves the warehouse and turns left out of the junction, thereby not crossing the central checkpoint. To my astonishment Commandos Elijah Dopo and Suehn Weah impound the car in the middle of the road, where there is no checkpoint, and demand to search the vehicle. I refuse categorically and start to complain. By this stage I am at the end of my tether. The commandos walk over to my vehicle, waving their guns and shouting, discussing my colour and organisation. Elijah Dopo pushes his fingers in my face. My last drop of patience goes and I aggressively bite his finger. A fight between us breaks out, Elijah Dopo is slammed on to the coal tar. This prompts an attack by ten to 15 commandos rushing from the gate. They assault me. My face is butted by a rifle and my clothes and UN armband are ripped off my body. One NPFL representative, Mr Johnson, tries to protect me.

'4.30 pm. County Commander Joe Doe arrives on the scene. He is accompanied by a senior NPFL soldier who is an assistant to Isaac Musah in Kakata. Joe Doe does not communicate with me. Instead his colleague approaches me and escorts me back to my house where papers are called for. I am advised that if I am faced with incidences of harassment and provocation I should seek to report the issue to the overall commander and not lose my temper. The matter is left to rest.

'5.00 pm. Two checkpoints appear 200 metres either side of the UN house.

'Friday Evening: As is the case for most nights in Zwedru there is continuous shooting. Between 10 pm and midnight we monitored the level of shooting: over 200 shots fired in two hours!

'Saturday morning, 14 December: A decision is taken to stay in Grand Gedeh until Tuesday morning so that all the food can be distributed. I had wanted to leave Zwedru immediately but I knew that this would have jeopardised any chance of food reaching the outside villages and towns.

'Tuesday Morning 17th December: The UN along with AICF, our medical and supplementary feeding partners, officially pull out of Grand Gedeh, and close this operation.

'I recommend that the UN should not return to Grand Gedeh until:

(a) the commandos involved in the harassment and molestation of UN workers are removed from the region.

(b) the NPFL respect the status of the UN and abide by the operational agreement reached between UN and he NPFL/NPRAG.

(c) the checkpoint in the middle of Zwedru is removed.

(d) the demand that all local casual labourers employed by the UN have ID cards is dropped.

'Below is a list of commandos who are known to have been highly destructive and belligerent and whose names are Elijah Dopo; Suehn Weah; Vomah Vaue; Sam Dahn; Commander Perry; Michael Dahn, (also involved in the theft of MSF medical supplies). There are other commandos who I am easily able to identify but their names are unknown to me.'

The report is classic Seán. First of all, he makes the undiplomatic mistake of owning up to losing his temper and biting the finger of one of the men who wanted to stop the UN's food from reaching the starving. A more cynical operator would have described the incident as an unprovoked assault. Secondly – and this is something that anyone who knew Seán would have been very proud of him for – despite being badly beaten up and the intimidation of the firing into the night near the UN compound, he chose to stay in Zwedru for four nights to ensure that all the food and equipment got to the starving Krahn people in the outlying villages. This decision required the true definition of courage: grace under pressure.

One of the very first people to get to Seán after he had been beaten up was Michael Emery. He hurried to Seán's bedside to find him entirely wrapped up in bandages like an Egyptian mummy. Fearing the worst, Michael said: 'Seán, are you all right, mate?' To his chagrin, he saw the mummy quiver with laughter. The bandages were yet another of Seán's outrageous stunts. But he *had* been badly beaten up, was heavily bruised about the body and sported a superb black eye for weeks afterwards.

Seán's beating had consequences for Michael too. After it happened the news got on the BBC's Focus On Africa programme at 5.05 and apparently about 5.20 the head of Charles Taylor's army turned up at Michael's office in Gbarnga, wielding a whip and asking for Michael because he was the only person the man knew. Michael wasn't there – he was in Monrovia – so Taylor's henchman sentenced him to 25 lashes in absentia because 'the white man had been lying to the BBC'. As a result, Michael wasn't allowed to go back to Gbarnga for three weeks and therefore the relief programmes were wound down. That was the effect a flippant report could have on the relief workers in the field. Michael felt that if something was going to hit a really sensitive nerve, then maybe it was best not to report it if there were people in the field. Had Michael been in Gbarnga, he would have had the 25 lashes administered to him. It would have been a good story for the grandchildren, but thankfully he wasn't there.

After this incident, the UN and all the other aid agencies pulled out from up-country Liberia, effectively Taylor-held territory.

In January, Seán himself went home to White Picketts for a short break where he relaxed, ran us ragged and picked up various threads of correspondence with friends from around the world.

One letter, to his fellow aid worker Paul McDermott, described the beating incident and Seán's misery at his new and unexpected predicament. He was particularly outraged that the NPFL had declared on Gbarnga radio that they had never harassed any relief workers. What was more, they were still in the possession of 13 relief vehicles, stolen by the rebels. Seán had supposedly 'bitten off' a soldier's finger – 'not surprising anyway, because I had a reputation,' he wrote. 'When I write this in the calmness and security of England it seems just ludicrous, but it's all true.'

In the meantime, Gbarnga had clearly opened the roads, moved most of the checkpoints, allowed ECOMOG to enter but still had full control.

Seán was worried that Taylor would win a fraudulent election – time would tell.

When Seán looked back, he realised he could have been shot, but as he said, 'When your temper pops, that's it!' He was supposed to have another six months' contract with UN, but didn't see how that would be possible now, though he was confident things would work out somehow. Michael was due back in England on 10 February and was then going on to Australia. Seán wondered if he would come back.

It was a personal blow to Seán to have been declared persona non grata, especially by a lawless, corrupt authority whose legacy was one of murder, persecution and tyranny. On a psychological level he suffered greatly, having been badly beaten in an area where gun law was the only respected authority. He had been lucky that time. Had the incident gone another way, it could have cost him his life. Most of all, it was the injustice of being expelled which preyed on his mind.

However, a short break in England enabled him to come to terms with the fatuity of this action. His sisters noticed the difference in him. Theresa recalls that Seán would talk a bit about it, but if he saw her getting upset he would stop. He would always play it down, never say what had really happened or how dangerous the situation really was.

After Zwedru, he told us that he was now 95 per cent stubborn rather than 100 percent.

DESTINY SOMALIA

That Christmas of 1991 – Seán's last in Liberia – had been a special one for the small group of aid workers in Monrovia. The workers for the Irish charity Goal prepared a Christmas dinner for 18 people. Michael Emery developed a game called 'The Beer Hunter' based on the Russian roulette game in the 'The Deer Hunter', which they played late into Christmas Day. For New Year's Eve Seán – who had been confined to Monrovia after the beating incident – organised a toga party for around 100 people in the house he and Michael shared, nicknamed 'The Temple of Doom'. The whole evening was authentically Roman, with everyone in togas apart from the goat on the spit and the American defence attaché, Bob Parnell, who dressed up in his tropical white uniform bedecked with his medals. The US Marine corporals, Eric and Danny, came in Californian togas made from psychedelic material and carrying surf boards under their arms. Michael came as a centurion, though his costume looked a little battle-worn as he had fallen in a ditch while running for a radio message at the UN compound.

Seán was now stuck in an office in Monrovia, which he hated. He didn't improve matters by refusing to answer his new call sign, Delta Three, preferring to stick with Shamrock. One of his jobs was to set up a new electoral control commission, which he attacked with his usual vigour. But the real work was to be done out in the hinterland – from where he had been banned by Taylor's 'government'. Also, as the war petered out, there was much less killing going on and the population began to recover from serious malnutrition, so there was less work for aid workers to carry out.

That June, Seán tried to organise the trials for the Liberian Olympics. Gerry Naughton, a young volunteer for the Salesians, remembers that Seán had been on the radio that week advertising the search for Liberia's fastest man and woman. About 30 participants had registered. Most of them were not trained athletes – there were few enough of them in war-torn Liberia – but had been attracted to the advert. There were to be four events, the 100m, the 400m, the 800m and the long jump, but in Seán's words the 'Blue Riband' event was the 100m. Seán brought the marshals he had been coaching to officiate. They all had the same T-shirts and armbands saying 'race official'. The sun came out, the track dried. Everything was ready to start.

Seán had his megaphone and was down on the track waiting to get going when it became apparent there was an internal wrangle taking place. One official of the Liberian Track and Field Federation complained that the trial should not take place because they already had some trained athletes who should get the three available places to go to the Olympics. Though Seán tried hard to pacify and placate, not even his charm and authority could make a breakthrough. The man complaining said that if they started the races, he would lie down on the track. Seán gave him a deadline for when the first race would start, but the deadline passed and still nothing had been resolved. Eventually, the meet was called off. Seán announced through the megaphone that all the competitors should go to this troublemaker for their money back. He told the people in charge that he was having no more to do with them, whether they rescheduled the trials or not. In the end, the trials never took place. Instead the three places were given to three Liberian boxers who arrived in Barcelona late and were disqualified before the competition started.

It was the only time Gerry saw Seán defeated. 'He looked really exasperated and frustrated. The whole business was like the Liberian problem in microcosm.'

Seán used to spend a lot of time helping the street kids and orphans based at the Matadi project in Monrovia. Typically, what sticks in the minds of his friends is not the good work, but the fun.

Gerry Naughton recalls one spectacular moped race from the Matadi complex to the UN compound on 8th Street. He and Seán had a race back, and Seán was wearing his wicker hat because his helmet made him look like a human cannonball. His moped was an older model than Gerry's so he had an advantage. To get the better of his friend, Seán took short cuts along the backstreets. Gerry was going along Tubman Boulevard when Seán suddenly shot out of a side-street ahead of him. He was jubilant because there was hardly any time before they got to 8th Street and their side of the road was packed with traffic. Gerry had to cross over onto the other side of the road against the oncoming traffic to beat Seán, which he only just did.

Seán left Monrovia on 9 July 1992, never to return. Nonetheless his love for Liberia, its young people and its culture did not diminish, and was evident from his letters to Michael and two of his students. Quite simply, he was homesick for Liberia. 'Once you leave you begin to realise the extent of your attachment to that bloody place,' he wrote. 'It's the people that make everything. I miss Emmanuel and the lads a lot'.

The past year had allowed him to get close to, share with and understand the Liberians to a degree that white people are not normally fortunate enough to attain.

To John, one of his Liberian students, he wrote that the best cure for his pining was to have a Liberian Day, so he had written to lots of Liberians and sent their letters with a DHL pack to Michael, which made him feel much better. Knowing that John was interested in furthering his studies, Seán had also been making tentative enquiries about courses for overseas students at English universities.

He ended the letter on a poignant note. 'Liberians deserve better than the bunch of hooligans they have in power at the moment. I hope that some good will turn out in the end. If all goes well next month I think I would like to try for Somalia. It sounds desperate, the people are really suffering, but I reckon it's the sort of work that will suit me. I will keep you informed of my whereabouts and I am confident that eventually we will meet up again, maybe in Liberia.'

Seán also wrote to another Liberian friend, Richard, telling him about his trip to the BBC in London, where he met Ofeibea. They went around the city for the day, and Ofeibea later took Seán to the Focus on Africa studio, where he had a good chat with Robin White and Elizabeth O'Heany. Robin wanted to interview him on the state (condition) of Liberia, but Seán refused because he knew he would say only bad things about Taylor and the NPFL, thereby getting the rest of the UN in trouble.

Seán began to talk more and more about Somalia. The pictures of the starving children were on the television screens night after night. As a family we discussed this assignment and the danger involved. It was a difficult period for him as he was anxious to move away from areas of conflict, but he saw the need to assist in Somalia and felt bound to do his bit. He would leave on 9 September

The news naturally worried us. Worse, I was undergoing a personal crisis right at the time when he needed my support. Instead the roles were reversed. Seán was for me a tower of strength, my friend, who helped me through the most difficult period of my life. Ever 'the organiser', he arranged for us to spend some time together in Guernsey before his departure for Somalia. It was an active time with daily cross-country runs at six every morning, followed by hours of tennis, swimming and cycling before collapsing into the pub for a gallon of beer at lunchtime. Evenings were spent over a leisurely meal, several bottles of wine and some serious talking.

On the last day I stood alone at the top of the cliff-face overlooking Petit Point. I watched Seán climb down the small wooden steps which weaved their way through the hillside foliage down to the sea. He was dwarfed on the seashore as he walked towards the ocean leaving his footsteps in the soft sand. The incoming tide ebbed its way around the rocks and carried him out into the white surf. The yellow streaks of the sinking sun cast shadows over the water's edge and blended into a kaleidoscope of colours to cast a spell upon the scene below. High above in the clear blue sky a sea bird soared effortlessly over the hillside. The cool evening breeze twisted and turned the yellow gorse bushes into a frenzy. The bird swooped down, gliding past me as it viewed me curiously and rose again with a powerful stroke of its wings, reminding me that some greater power ruled over us. What prospects lay ahead for Seán in Somalia?

Suddenly he was in front of me, refreshed by the sea. 'A couple of nice brandies and a good bottle of wine will do the trick now, Dad,' he said.

I handed him a small twig in the shape of a crucifix which I had absently plucked from a branch on the hillside. 'Hang on to this. You'll need it in that bloody place you're going to next week,' I said. He looked at me, smiled, accepted it and made no comment.

We left the hilltop in silence.

THERESA:
THE DYING OF THE LIGHT

Dis alter visum
(Virgil, Aeneid, 11, 428)
'The Gods thought otherwise.'

Winter 1992. It had been a terrible few months on the personal front and I was determined to get away from it all for Christmas. Seán had been over in the summer but I had a real urge to see him again, so I decided to try and meet up with him in Nairobi when he was on his five-day stopover from Somalia. However, I had no luck booking flights – everything was either overbooked or way out of my price range so in the end I decided to have a quiet Christmas at home and then go skiing with friends in the New Year.

Just before Christmas, on a whim Dad decided to look up BA staff travel availability to Nairobi. Surprisingly, considering the trouble I'd had, there were four available seats going out on the 24th and returning New Year's Eve, coinciding exactly with Seán's leave. On a split second decision we decided to go. It meant we could all have Christmas together – an increasingly rare event as we got older. So we cancelled the parties, Mum put the turkey in the freezer and instead of singing hymns at midnight mass, we found ourselves on our way to Africa.

Seán met us at the hotel on Boxing Day. He was, as usual, full of life as he burst into the hotel lobby, expertly manoeuvring his case through the revolving doors.

We had a really wonderful holiday together – it was one of those special times. But Seán wasn't his usual self. There was a tension and preoccupation in him that I'd never seen before. I put it down to the stress of Somalia, while my parents anxiously questioned him about how safe it was for him to be there.

As for Seán and me, we got on brilliantly. Somehow the holiday marked a turning point in our relationship. The competitive elements that had characterised our childhood and early adulthood had finally retreated. I remember feeling grateful that we could at last let the love and closeness we shared come through. All the same, he still kept imitating my laugh! One afternoon Tania, Seán and I went shopping in Nairobi market. The city was unusually empty and quiet because the elections were on and there was the possibility of trouble. This made the little clusters of street children lurking on corners all the more noticeable. As we walked Seán started talking about their growing number and how much he'd like to set up a centre for them in Nairobi based on Don Bosco schools.

Uncannily, as we walked the streets, children seemed drawn to us and we soon had a large group trailing behind. Seán stopped at a newspaper kiosk to buy a large packet of sweets. He winked at Tania and me, his eyes gleaming mischievously, and as we walked on, he took one of the shiny wrapped sweets and wiggled it tantalizingly at the children from behind his back.

As if their eyes were radar-sensitive, a bunch of kids jumped delightedly on him and scuffled with each other as they tried to grab the sweet, which had flown up in the air.

It was an amusing sight – Seán with his bandy legs in shorts and old loose docksiders ambling down the road with kids joyously pouncing on his hands every ten or twelve yards. We were all enjoying the game but every now and again Seán would stop and make the children do some jobs, like pick up rubbish from the street. Tania and I were really annoyed with him, thinking he was acting like some big white chief; but he explained that it was his attempt, albeit a crude one, to try and show the children they mustn't expect anything for nothing. He talked with real feeling and exasperation, saying how destructive he believed the 'hand-out' mentality was becoming in Africa.

The discussion was broken by one little boy who had crept to my side and was looking up at me pleadingly. He was only about four and too young to have any chance of winning the battle of the sweets. I gave him one and he carefully undid the wrapper with his chubby brown hands, hiding behind me out of view of the others. His little dirty face and gentle brown eyes were so endearing I couldn't help but give him a cuddle and he looked at me incredulously for a moment before skipping off, the sweet safely lodged in the bulge of his cheek.

We wandered into the market and pottered about, bargaining and marvelling at the beautiful soap stone figures and wood carvings, and generally enjoying the hurly burly atmosphere. Then, just as we were about to leave I felt a tap at my side – it was the little boy I had met earlier. I looked at him knowingly and reached into Seán's bag for another sweet. He took it but this time didn't seem that interested in it and continued staring up at me with his beautiful, innocent eyes. Understanding the value of sweets in street child mentality, I was baffled by his behaviour for a minute but then it dawned on me what he had really come back for – another cuddle!

The last day of the holiday arrived. That evening we went for a final celebration dinner. Inevitably, the conversation turned to Somalia and the tasks that lay ahead of Seán. Dad grilled him about the wisdom of continuing in such a dangerous place, asking him how he felt about the murder of the five American nuns in Liberia some five weeks previously. Seán was visibly pained by their fate; they had been his close friends. He recalled their sense of fun, commitment and compassion, and the wonderful contribution they had made to Africa over the past 35 years. 'It's just so difficult to accept they're dead,' he said.

'But that's just the point, Seán,' said Mum, 'they are. Do you really think it's worth it?' And then she asked him what he thought happens to us after death.

Seán, realising that the subject was getting a bit heavy, closed the conversation. 'I have no concept of what happens when we die, all I know is that while my heart beats I want to make the most of every minute I'm alive.'

Then he was on his feet, having a joke with the waiter, ordering more wine.

The following morning there was a lot of false hilarity as we packed our suitcases into the waiting cab. No one liked saying goodbye. I gave Seán a hug and, embarrassed to cry in front of him, squashed myself into the car with my head down, trying to hide my tears.

There was an eerie silence as the taxi pulled away from the rank. I turned to look at Seán out of the corner of the back window. He was on his own, in shorts and a white cotton jumper, distractedly kicking a stone down the steps of our hotel. It's my last memory of him.

Back in England, I managed to make a New Year's Eve party, squeeze in a trip to the theatre and then on Saturday 2 January set off to Geneva for a week's skiing. I remember thinking how great life was: two weeks of constant pleasure. It was too good to be true.

The journey to the ski resort, Meribel, turned out to be a complete nightmare – I've never known so much to go wrong in one day. It was as if everything was conspiring against me, trying to bring me to a standstill. As the day progressed I felt more and more sluggish and flat. Little did I know that, by the time I got to Meribel, Seán was already dead.

It wasn't until Sunday afternoon, 18 hours after Seán had been murdered, that I got the news. That hour in my life seems set in slow motion. I was having tea in the chalet when a note came to ring my parents immediately.

I remember being irritated at the thought of going out in the cold again to the phone box. 'This had better be important,' I thought as I tackled the icy hill.

My parents' number was engaged for the next hour and I began to worry. Eventually I got through and was surprised to hear the voice of Greg, a family friend, at the end of the line.

'Oh, hi Greg,' I said. 'Why are you answering the phone?' to which he replied urgently: 'What's your number, Theresa?' and then: 'She's on Dermot, I've got her on!'

'What's wrong, Greg?' I said, confused.

'First – give – me – your – number – Theresa.' He was very assertive and I felt a flutter of anxiety in my chest.

'What the hell's wrong, Greg?' I shouted and then heard Dad's voice at the end of the line, croaking and weak.

'Christ, what's wrong, Dad?' I said, shaking.

'Oh Theresa, darling!' he said. 'Theresa, darling, you're going to have to be very, very strong...' He paused. 'It's Seán...he's been shot.'

'Oh my God! Shot? Where? Is he hurt? Oh my God, is he all right?'

'He's dead!' Dad blurted out and burst into tears.

Dead? Jesus Christ, dead? No. No. I couldn't stop screaming – I felt the force of the shock explode in my stomach, buckling me over.

My sister's voice on the phone pulled me to my senses – she was saying bravely and calmly: 'It's all right, Theresa, try and calm yourself a bit – it's all right, I was like that. Try and calm yourself.' She was being so brave, really trying to comfort me and I remember thinking: 'God, I've got to pull myself together.' It was the worst moment of my life.

The first six hours after I'd heard were dreadful – I just remember feeling completely empty and dead. I'd never experienced the death of someone close before and had always hoped there would be some sense of something, not this deep black nothingness.

My friends were incredibly gentle and kind to me and I was so grateful for them. I went to bed that night but sleep didn't come – I remember thinking: shit, how am I going to get through the next week, facing the pain of my family, the funeral, burying Seán's body? The thought was unbearable and I felt I was in a mire of blackness.

It was probably the contrast with my own bleakness but I remember an image of Seán coming to me that night – he was silhouetted in thousands of diamonds of bright white light, somersaulting in the air with the same panache and delight he used to have when he'd mastered some new magic trick. He seemed to dismiss my misery and was saying: 'It's brilliant, Theresa – it's really brilliant.' It was followed by very powerful feelings of love and peace and I found myself being reconnected to Seán, something which has never gone.

But the words 'Seán's dead, Seán's dead' kept ringing in my ears for days afterwards and at times the pain of it was almost too much.

On the plane next day, the stewardess dished out the newspapers. A picture on the front of *The Daily Mail* caught my eye – it was me and Seán in my parents' kitchen in Yateley. Reading the article, I learned that Seán had been targeted. I was shocked. Up till then I'd assumed he had been caught in the crossfire and it was very painful to think that someone had deliberately wanted to hurt him.

Back home in Yateley we were engulfed by love and kindness from family, friends, neighbours and even strangers. Every day sackfuls of letters arrived. They said such lovely things about Seán, their words of sympathy really helped. Through it all I found I was beginning to learn something – the true value of compassion.

Seán's body was flown home four days after he died. I found that difficult and couldn't go to the airport to meet it like the rest of my family; I couldn't bear the contrast of a dead body instead of Seán, full of life, buzzing out of the arrivals gate in his beige khaki trousers and blue and white stripey shirt.

He was always excited to be home.

Last time I'd picked him up on his return from Liberia I remember him relaxing back in the seat of my bashed-up old car and looking with pleasure at the sprawling mass of building work and usual mayhem at Heathrow Airport.

'Oh, it's nice to be back to a bit of law and order,' he sighed as I accidentally cut up a white escort. 'You really appreciate it, you know, the sense of safety and order there is in England,' he added just as the escort driver, now turned maniac bull, undertook me, his two-fingered hand held menacingly in the air.

We made it home and drew up in front of the familiar stone front of White Picketts. Seán's eyes were bright with anticipation. Mum came out through the porch, Tania dancing behind her. They'd made themselves look nice for him. Mum was relieved to see him and smiled as she cuddled him, tears glinting slightly with a kind of suppressed emotion.

The cooker was a bubbling mass of saucepans and there were fresh apple pies on the sideboard. 'Mmm, steak,' Seán said as he poked the slab of fresh red meat lying raw in the frying pan.

'What have you been eating, Seán?' Mum said, surveying him worriedly – although he hadn't lost as much weight as usual.

'You'll never guess,' he said, 'we've been having the most brilliant meals.' His eyes lit up at the thought of it. 'The British Embassy chef's been cooking for us – when the embassy closed Michael found him and persuaded him to cook for us at the UN compound. He's been making some wonderful concoctions with the army rations.'

Seán loved his food, and by the end of a holiday at home he'd invariably have gained a stone or so. He loved going back to Africa a bit fatter, loved the way the Liberians would slap him around the tummy and congratulate him on his hefty new figure. They have a completely different attitude where weight is concerned – basically, the fatter the better. It's a sign of wealth.

He pulled out some rather dubious-looking garments – he fancied himself as a bit of a fashion designer and cheap African tailors provided him with the ideal opportunity.

'These are for you,' he said to Tania and me, oozing enthusiasm as he passed us some green tie-dyed material cut into triangles.

'What are they?' I said.

'Dresses, of course, you idiot,' he replied indignantly. 'Personally designed by me,' he added, as is if this would make then wearable. Tania tried hers on and it hung like a limp dustbin liner.

'Seán's amazing fashion sense,' she said and we all had a laugh.

'Ah, you've got no taste,' he said, unperturbed, pulling out his own 'personally designed' shirts and made-to-match Islamic hats, holding them up to himself and lovingly stroking the colourful African prints.

My reminiscence was broken by the crackle of Dad's white Sierra drawing slowly up our curved drive. His face was blank, expressionless at the wheel. Mum was sitting next to him, her small, fragile body overwhelmed with the burden of it all. They sat there motionless and exhausted for a while and then Tania got out of the back, her usual bouncy step now deliberate and stiff, her normal bright smiley eyes dulled with sadness. I felt the swell of tears surge up in my eyes again and that crushing pain in my heart.

Caroline Tanner was with them. She'd flown back with Seán's body. She had been there just after he was shot and had escorted the body all the way back from Kismayo to London. It wasn't easy for her, Seán was one of her best friends, but I was so grateful she'd been able to stay with him.

Caroline told us exactly what had happened. Seán had been hit from behind: one shot to the head, two in the back. It was so quick, he wouldn't have known anything about it. It was a great relief to know he hadn't suffered.

The following evening, Wednesday, was the wake. I was apprehensive about it. I'd never been to one before and didn't know how I'd cope. I was grateful for the friends and family who were visiting the house; it took my mind off things.

The evening was looming closer. I kept trying to block it out. I didn't want to go through this – another hurdle to face.

Dad came back from the hospital. He had just formally identified Seán's body. He looked very sad, his hands slunk deep in his jacket pockets, his head drooped, big swollen bags under his tired eyes. My heart bled for him.

'He's in a bit of a mess, Threes,' he said, shaking his head miserably. 'I'm debating whether to cover his face tonight before the others see him.' I noticed the wet tears on his cheekbones.

I agreed to go in early and decide with him. I was frightened of what I would see but didn't want to be spared the facts – I wanted to be entirely satisfied that Seán hadn't suffered.

Early that evening, Dad and I drove the few miles to the chapel of rest. We parked outside – the window was dressed with gravestones and silver cremation caskets. I was surprised I hadn't noticed the place before, tucked next to a hairdressers I often visit.

We went through the front door and into a waiting room. It was small and dark. The sides were lined with low chairs covered in red velvet cloth. The funeral director greeted us. He was old and bent, dressed in a dark suit and moved very slowly, but he was kind and I appreciated his respectfulness. He led us into a room at the back. There was an open coffin and in it, dressed in a suit, lay Seán.

I peered over the side to get a closer look at his face and a knife of shock ran through me. The whole side of his temple had been blown away, exposing a deep raw concavity on the left side of his head. I took a sharp intake of breath. 'God, it's bad, Dad,' I said. I hadn't been prepared to see this.

Dad looked at Seán and we agreed it would be best to cover his injury before the others saw him.

He then left to pick up Mum and Tania and I was grateful to have a few minutes alone to say goodbye to my brother. I stroked the side of his hand; it was cold and rubbery. His face was expressionless, and I felt myself start to sink again into that abyss. But I was stopped by a sudden realisation. I realised that this wasn't Seán at all. Everything that was Seán had left – all that energy, enthusiasm, *joie de vivre*, had gone. But not gone in the sense of vanished: it had gone somewhere else. His body had died but deep inside me I knew he hadn't. The pain and sadness lifted, there was a real peace and beauty in the room, which passed over and steadied me.

Dad returned to place a cloth over the damaged area on Seán's face. Mum followed. 'Just like the dream,' she said as she gently touched Seán's shoulder. They were very calm and dignified, the peace was touching them too. They both sat at the top of the coffin as our relatives and Seán's closest friends came in to pay their last respects.

Then it was Thursday. The day before the funeral. Time was moving us on. Friends and relatives were flying in from all over the world and Michael was coming in from Australia. The house was a whirr of activity, the phone ringing continuously, arrangements being made to meet people at airports and stations. The doorbell was buzzing with relatives and neighbours offering to put people up. Auntie Theresa was busily organising the funeral service. What readings? Which hymns? Tea, wine and food were constantly on the go.

I retreated up to my bedroom for a few hours' break – a pile of neatly ironed clothes had been placed on my bed by a neighbour who was taking care of our laundry. I was touched again by the kindnesses we were being shown. Seán's laptop was in my room – it had been flown back with his body. I needed to get my mind off things, so I thought I might as well try and get it to work. I unzipped the black PVC casing and pulled it out. Hunting around for the instructions manual, I came across Seán's 1992 diary. It was tatty and well-used with the spine missing and a picture of an African mother and child sellotaped to the front.

There were several personal cards stapled to the inside – journalists, UN staff, army commanders, Liberian politicians, Catholic newspapers, NGOs, telephone numbers of Salesian priests. I skimmed through it, feeling slightly uncomfortable. It was his private business but I desperately wanted some contact with him. The pages were covered with plans for emergency food distribution – quick calculations of rice, beans, oil and fish requirements, hastily drawn route maps and names of rebel commandos he had to negotiate with.

There were also rough notes on the talks he gave about Liberia. It was difficult to make head or tail of them but three words were written in clear red letters repetitively: 'Commitment to Humanity.'

I felt sick. I held the book close. This was Seán.

The phone rang constantly, hundreds of different people were coming to the funeral. A call came in from UNICEF Somalia to tell us that some of the elders in Kismayo had organised a march through the town in protest over Seán's killing. Many people had turned out. I was struck by such integrity and bravery. Somalia was a hot seat – they could have put their own lives at risk.

That evening Michael Emery and Ofeibea Quist-Arcton, the BBC's West African correspondent, arrived. It was good to see them. Michael was strong, swallowing back the tears as he greeted us. I was glad to meet Ofeibea; I had heard a lot about her from Seán. She had great presence, sweeping into the house in beautiful African robes covered by a warm winter coat, her handsome Ghanaian face beneath a chic-looking Islamic hat.

She had to go back to London for the night and I went to the car to see her off. Before she got in, she turned to me and pressed a beautiful silver bangle into my hand.

'Courage,' she said, 'courage' as her deep brown eyes poured strength into mine.

Friday morning. The funeral was at 12 o'clock. Tania, Mum and I were trying to decide what to wear. I didn't want to wear black – too miserable. Seán wouldn't have liked it so I opted for a blue wool suit.

I went downstairs and someone put some tea and toast in front of me. I couldn't eat – everything was going dream-like again. A hearse and four or five black funeral cars drew up outside our house. They looked so morbid. Was this really happening to us?

Dad guided us into the cars and we were driven slowly up to the church. The road seemed silent – everything was going in slow motion. We arrived at the church. There were police and film crew everywhere, it was confusing.

We sat for a moment before we got out of the car and I felt myself take hold. I looked at the silver bangle and touched it.

'Courage,' I said to myself, 'courage.'

The church was packed. People stood in the aisles and poured out of the porch, their faces filled with sympathy. Seán's coffin was in the centre draped in the blue and white UNICEF flag. Across to the left, I could see a group of my friends. They were smiling at me, willing compassion across to me and my heart lit. To the right a pew of dark faces stood out – they were Somali refugees based in London. I felt the ugly knot of prejudice melt away.

The mass was beautiful. Seán would have been proud.

Coping with Seán's death has been a long and difficult process but by allowing myself time to grieve I find it is copeable. I miss Seán and I miss what could have been. It's been hard learning to live without him. However, there is one recurring thought that has always kept me going. I know that when it's my time to die, he'll be over there, on the other side, waiting.

MAUREEN:
A BORROWED JEWEL

Summer 1992 was a terrible time for our family. Dermot and I were experiencing serious personal problems. At that time Seán's contract with UNICEF in Monrovia had come to an end and he had decided to come and stay at home with us for a few months to try and help us through. He was a great support, as were our other two children. His next posting was UNICEF Somalia. Naturally, I felt worried about the life he had chosen, working in dangerous parts of Africa.

Somalia was very similar to Liberia. I never discussed my anxieties with him. In motherhood there is an innate desire to protect, cherish and hold on to that which has been born of us. The inevitable realisation that your child must leave the nest and embrace the world for good or bad is not easy. I found it extremely difficult. Seán too must have understood the bond which we have with our children, as before he left for Somalia he gave his father and me a small gift, a little book called *The Prophet* by the Eastern mystic, Kahlil Gibran. Written inside were the words 'To Mom and Dad with love from Seán. You have achieved wonderfully the message on page 13.' It read as follows:

'Your children are not your children,
They are the sons and daughters of life's longing for itself.
They come through you but not from you,
And though they are with you yet they belong not to you.
You may give them your love but not your thoughts,
For they have their own thoughts,
You may house their bodies but not their souls,
For their souls dwell in the houses of tomorrow
Which you cannot visit, not even in your dreams.
You may strive to be like them, but seek not to make them like you
For life goes not backwards nor tarries with yesterday.
You are the bows from which your children as living arrows are sent forth.
The Archer sees the mark upon the path of the infinite
And He bends you with His might that His arrow may go swift and far.

Let your bending in the Archer's hand be for gladness;
For even as he loves the arrow that flies, He loves also the bow that is stable.'

As I watched my children grow I often wondered how I could ever cope if I lost a child, and shuddered at the thought.

Then my worst fear was a reality.

At 6 pm on the evening of 2 January 1993 we received the shattering news that Seán had been assassinated. That evening is embedded in my memory forever. It was like any other day until the telephone rang. The voice at the other end asked to speak to Mr Devereux. There was something in his manner that put me on my guard. I had only the briefest of moments to think like this. From the shock on Dermot's face I knew something terrible had happened. His voice was trembling as I heard the words; 'How badly is he hurt?' Panic-stricken, I put my ear to the telephone and heard an Australian accent. The voice of Mark Sterling, UNICEF representative in Somalia, was saying, 'I'm sorry, mate, it's all over. Seán was shot by a gunman 30 minutes ago. I'm sorry. We are in a state of shock here.' We clung to each other and stood rooted to the floor.

Tania, our youngest, had only just left the house with a friend to celebrate a 21st birthday party. Theresa had left that morning to join a friend on a skiing holiday in Switzerland. I cannot express the torturous anxiety I felt at the thought of having to break the terrible news to them. Dermot and I just clung to each other and wandered around the house, saying: 'This can't be true, we were with him yesterday.' The television was on and we overheard the evening news. 'British aid worker Seán Devereux shot dead in Somalia.' Seán's face flashed across the TV screen. I stared at the screen. I thought all this was happening around us but not to me. We were in shock, unable to function. Family and friends gathered around us very quickly. The house was soon full of people. The full magnitude of our situation began to sink in that night, as well as the realisation that we were going to go through this grief in public. I was terrified that Theresa might hear the shattering news before we could reach her.

The next few days were very unreal: making arrangements for Seán's body to be flown home for burial, the phone constantly ringing, friends arriving from different parts of the world. The day before the funeral, Seán's body was received into our parish church, St Swithun's in Yateley.

As I knelt beside his coffin I had many conflicting emotions towards my own religion; but my faith was something to hold on to, or maybe something that held on to me. My conversation with God was full of anger that Seán had been wrenched from us in such a cruel way, murdered by another human being. He'd had the courage to live what he believed in and had responded to the call by trying to improve the pitiful suffering of mankind, feed the hungry, clothe the naked and help people who were less fortunate than him.

My faith was really tested during the service that evening when Father Lawrence read a passage from an ancient tale of faith: 'The son of a wise Rabbi died while he was away from home. Knowing how deeply he loved his son, the Rabbi's wife decided to wait for a while before breaking the tragic news to her husband. When he came home he asked for his son repeatedly. His wife always replied, "He is not here now." Then she sat him down and said, "You are a very wise and learned man, help me to find some answers to this unbearable problem. If you were lent a precious jewel and told you could enjoy it as long as it was in your keeping, would you be able to argue with the lender if he asked for it back?" Her husband thought for a moment and replied, "Certainly not." His wife then led him to the bedroom and said, "God wanted his jewel back." '

People who are so close to their God and have such deep faith are very fortunate. They are sure God has a greater plan, and while they grieve for their child they are relieved of a sense of futility. They can ask, 'Why did it happen to me?' without destroying themselves emotionally. They can give themselves many answers. At that stage my faith had not penetrated to that deeper layer of consciousness. I was unable to see any higher plan, but the message that my child was lent to me became very clear. As I knelt by Seán's coffin I noticed a small card stuck to the side. It was a little prayer from my dear friend Cynthia Collins:

'Grieve not for me but more for those who stay behind, bound by longings for which the fruit is sorrow. For what confidence have we in life when death is ever at hand, even if I were to return to my kindred by reason of affection? Yet we should be divided in the end by death. The meetings and partings of living things is as if clouds, having come together, drift apart again or as when the leaves are parted from the trees. There is nothing we can call our own in a union that is just a dream.'

Somehow this prayer comforted me, and in a strange way I could hear Seán speaking to me.

People who die young leave a warm glow in the hearts of those who love them. It is as if their candle, because it burns for such a short time, glows brightest of all. Seán was so much part of us, having to accept that he had gone was more than I could bear. It was as if the sun had disappeared from the sky. I felt a great pulsating wound as I dragged myself around. It felt as if there was a huge hole in my chest, as though my rib cage had opened up and the wind was blowing through. I was convinced people passing by could see it. I learned what the cliché 'broken heart' meant. When your child dies you reach the depth of your sorrow, and my grief was compounded by the realisation that the connecting link between Theresa and Tania was gone. They had lost a treasured brother, and I felt helpless to support them.

After this profound loss I had a tendency to idealise Seán, for it is often the child who is far away, sick or no longer with us that we seem to treasure most. This emotional imbalance was soon corrected by Tania's sobering remarks. She would say, 'Are we talking about Saint Seán again?' We were all well aware of his exuberance and energy and the chaos he'd often caused. He had certainly been no saint.

For a long while our family was immobilised. Resources of strength and comfort ordinarily available to us no longer were. There were many turning points as I worked my way forward. I floated through the day mechanically, experiencing fluctuations of mood from utter desolation to hope.

There were days when I was not in reality. Sometimes when the phone rang I would lift the receiver and think I could hear Seán's cheerful voice on the other end; or I'd believe that if I got on a plane to Somalia, I would find him there, busily getting on with his life. My brain was telling me one thing, my heart was telling me something else. There were times when I wanted to keep the pain alive and I hugged my grief as if it was something to hold on to, a last link. I panicked when I laughed: how could I be separated from this great sadness? Worst of all, far worse than lying awake at night, were the mornings when remembering what had happened engulfed me like a tidal wave. I had to take certain steps daily to retain my meaningful life. Each morning I would dig deep inside myself and pray for a ration of courage for the day. I learned to find it through trying and sometimes failing. As with a muscle exercise, I gradually grew stronger.

The sudden loss also put an extra strain on our marriage. There is nothing much to give when you are both in deep emotional pain and feel equal grief. Dermot and I both felt so separate, unlike in earlier times when we'd laughed and shared many ups and downs together. I found that after this great tragedy in our lives, we mourned as individuals. In the back of our minds we'd believed we could always lean on each other, but you soon learn that you cannot lean on somebody bent double beneath their own burden. We expected too much of each other and received too little. We spent a lot of time lost in our private thoughts. There were questions we wanted to ask each other but chose not to, because the pain of answering them would outweigh any possible benefits. Yet we both knew well that to sit in misery would deny everything Seán had stood for, and throw it away as worthless. That would destroy the essence of Seán that still lived on in us more surely than the pain of his death.

As the days go by I think a lot about Seán, that wonderful interlude in my life, and somewhere deep inside me, in a place where I can only partly reach, I know he is continuing in the cycle of his life, and that is in the spiritual realm where he has always essentially been. We think we love people for their looks – their physical, sexual appeal – but when you analyse it, it is for their warmth, their humour, their intelligence, kindness, compassion. These are spiritual qualities, which Seán had in abundance, and even though he is not here, his presence is always with us.

I did have a glimpse of this in a dream just before Seán died. In the dream I saw Seán as a ball of energy. I observed this bright ball of energy release itself with great difficulty from his body. As the energy detached itself, it sat heavily by his head outside his physical body. Then another ball of energy, very light and free, descended at speed from the atmosphere. I recognised it as that of my mother, who'd died six years previously. She was calling Seán's name with sheer delight. It was as if she was coming for him. As she came closer the aura from her energy connected with Seán's energy and they both disappeared into the atmosphere together. At that moment I felt a distinct sense of separation from Seán. There was no sadness, no fear, no emotional torment: it was simply a natural process. His physical body seemed to remain by my bedside. I remember my words as I woke up: 'Seán, you are not on this earth any longer.' The dream was of such vividness that it remains with me in essence all the time.

I have thought a lot about this dream and I understand now that it was perhaps some sort of premonition, and also a reassurance that there is something greater than this earthly life, some other reality that we are not permitted to understand.

There were times when I didn't know how I would be able to stand the pain, but I believe in God and in the power of prayer, which helped me to regain some meaning in my life. I prayed a lot, which was better than the secret drinking I often felt like turning to, even though I felt God didn't really hear me. Why hadn't he been watching over Seán, who cared so much for others?

There is, of course, no soul-satisfying answer to this question. I view God differently now: I don't believe he hears individual prayers, but I see him more as a force which created this world and looks after its overall destiny, giving each human being a personal responsibility to respond to good and evil as his conscience allows him. In that God I live and breathe and have my being.

Strength and inspiration came gradually, not through any divine intervention but through the love, generosity and support of family and friends, and others who had been touched by Seán's spirit. Thousands of letters poured in from all over the world, many from people we had never met. Some opened up for me a whole new way of thinking. One in particular, written by a woman I will never know, still reaches out to me, reminding me that good prevails over evil and that we are all part of this family of man. These simple lines, together with a beautiful framed picture, arrived a few weeks after Seán's death:

'I saw on television the Devereux family, and read about your courageous selfless son, who cared so much for others. I have taken this picture down from my inglenook fireplace, where it hung for many years. I hope therefore that you will accept it with the love intended. Perhaps one day, at present beyond your view, it might just bring some measure of comfort. I pray that it will.

Sincerely, Nicola.'

The words in the picture were embroidered in beautiful silk: 'It is not the length of existence that counts, but what is achieved during that existence, however short.' This picture is now a treasured possession in my home. I often read it and it never fails to comfort me.

As long as I live I will feel deep sorrow that Seán is not on this earth. There are times, especially the good times, when I miss him terribly, but they are still good times. We share joys as a family that he did not live to see, but we still have joys. Never could I have envisioned us laughing and happy again, but through the sadness he has left me with a living source of energy which I find strengthening and reassuring. I have also become acutely aware that we do not have each other's friendship for very long.

I wanted to know everything about the place Seán had worked, see people he knew. Above all I wanted to talk to the security guards who had walked back with him to the UNICEF compound on that fatal evening. I wanted to know what his last words were. I had to wait for about a year before it was safe for me to make the trip. UNICEF had a plane in Nairobi to take me to Kismayo. It landed in Kismayo Airport with high security. I was surrounded by soldiers and guns. As I drove towards the town I was confronted with the pitiful suffering of the people in war-torn Somalia: vacant-eyed children, listless adults, bent dogs and thin chickens, sagging shacks and rubbish strewn everywhere.

Suddenly the driver pulled to a halt. Bill Candy of UNICEF security walked me towards the spot in the sand where Seán had died. This was where an assassin had stepped out from the shadows and shot him twice in

116

the back and once in the head. Just before Seán was shot, he'd seen an American helicopter flying overhead and said to the guards: 'We're OK now. We can at last get the food to the starving.'

I mustered up all the courage I could find. I felt the hard stab of the African sun in my eyes. With every step I became aware of the sand beneath my feet and the feel of my clothes against my skin. I had known Seán so deeply, all the memories came flooding back: Seán full of fun, Seán talking to you seriously, Seán dancing you off the floor.

A few barefoot Somali children gathered round me. They didn't really know my reason for being there but somehow I felt a little comforted by their innocent presence. They held my hand as I gazed into the sand.

I visited the feeding stations that Seán and Caroline had helped to set up. I cradled a two-year-old child who weighed less than a two-month-old baby, and felt helpless in the knowledge that the little bundle of bones was past all hope. Around me were others babies, toddlers and their parents, emaciated into virtual skeletons, all crying out for help. Yet they were the lucky ones, being loved and cared for by the brave aid workers.

I spent some time with the two Somali security guards who'd been with Seán when he died. Where were the US marines when he was walking back to the compound without adequate security? Their mandate was to protect the aid workers, of course it was.

Yet ultimately Seán had made a choice. In a country overrun with casual violence this was no chance shooting. For Seán was an outspoken aid worker who had openly criticised the actions of the local warlords to the international media, and had attacked the Mogadishu-based Marines for failing to intervene as an orgy of ethnic cleansing swept through Kismayo while they remained safely in Mogadishu. Faced with such atrocities and maybe careless of his own safety, Seán refused to remain silent or to couch his comments in the careful language of diplomacy, and for this he died.

The person who killed Seán is well known as the local hit-man in Kismayo. The fact that he is still free is wrong. Yet I have often thought about my feelings for this person. He is not entirely to blame. What about the person who ordered Seán's killing? What about *our* responsibility for the arms that are sold to these warlords for Western gain? What about UNICEF's responsibility for the security of its aid workers?

In life there seems to be a war between good and evil. You can be on the side of indifference, selfishness and greed or you can be on the side of generosity, love and courage. Seán was a witness to unbelievable acts of savagery and appalling evil; he saw the true effects of the arms trade.

He allied himself with what he thought was right. If his death can help to prevent the sales of weapons, especially to developing countries without democracy, it will at least seem less pointless.

I have always found the argument 'if we don't sell weapons to them, someone else will' quite shameful. I believe all war is evil, the very worst manifestation of human vice, though maybe some wars are less evil than others because they are fought for more humane reasons. War should, in any case, be the very last resort.

I pray that Seán's supreme sacrifice is not in vain, that his spirit will encourage us as a symbol of peace and inspire us with new hope.

Peace and justice are worthy of his fight.